THE GUERRILLA GUIDE TO
CREDIT REPAIR

THE GUERRILLA GUIDE TO
CREDIT REPAIR

HOW TO FIND OUT WHAT'S WRONG WITH YOUR CREDIT RATING—AND HOW TO FIX IT

TODD BIERMAN AND NATHANIEL WICE

ST. MARTIN'S PRESS
NEW YORK

Library of Congress Cataloging-in-Publication Data

Bierman, Todd.
    The Guerrilla Guide to Credit Repair / Todd Bierman and Nathaniel
Wice.
        p.   cm.
    ISBN 0-312-10734-X (pbk.)
    1. Consumer credit—United States.   I. Wice, Nathaniel.
    II. Title.
HG3756.U54B5   1994
332.7'43—dc20   93-43647
                                                                      CIP

10

Books are available in quantity for promotional or premium
use. Write to Director of Special Sales, St. Martin's Press,
175 Fifth Avenue, New York, N.Y. 10010, for information
on discounts and terms, or call toll-free (800) 221-7945. In
New York, call (212) 674-5151 (ext. 645).

Contents

NOTE TO THE READER   ix

INTRODUCTION

Overview of Credit Reporting   3
How Does This Book Work?   4
How Does Credit Repair Work?   4

GET YOUR CREDIT REPORT

Introduction   9
Letters:
    Buying Your Credit Report   12
    Requesting Your Free Credit Report   14
    Requesting Your Free Report If You Were
       Denied Credit   16
Advanced: Infiles   18
Advanced: Full Factual and Residential
       Mortgage Credit Reports   19

READ YOUR CREDIT REPORT

Introduction   23
Identifying Derogatory Items on:
    TRW Consumer Credit Report   24
    TRW Updated Credit Profile Disclosure
       Report   25
    TRW Infile   29
    TransUnion Consumer Relations Disclosure
       and Infile   32
    Equifax Credit History   36

REPAIR YOUR CREDIT REPORT

Introduction: Basic and Advanced   43
Basic Credit Bureau Disputes   43
    Step-by-Step Basic Credit Bureau Disputes   44
    Basic Dispute Flowchart for Disputing
       Three or Fewer Items   45

Basic Dispute Flowchart for Disputing
   Four or More Items   49
Standard Credit Bureau Stalling Techniques   53
Letters:
   Initial Dispute Letter   53
   Second-Notice Letter   58
   Demand Letter 1   60
   Demand Letter 2   63
   Secondary Dispute Letter   66
   FTC Dispute Letter   69
   If You Suspect That the Credit Bureau Is
      Confusing You with Someone Else   70
Advanced Credit Repair   70
   Introduction   70
   Choosing Basic or Advanced Techniques
      for Disputing a Derogatory Item   71
   Creditor Types:
      Retail Stores   74
      Banks and Mortgage Lenders   77
      Credit Cards   80
      Auto Loans   83
      Student Loan Agencies   85
      Medical   87
      Debt Collection Agencies   89
      Public Records   92
   Notes on Verbal Negotiations   93
   Full Factual Glossing   97
   Letters:
      Restrictively Endorsed Settlement   98
      Agreement to Clear Collection Account   100
      Debt Schedule Settlement   102
      Student Loan Forbearance Notification   104
      Advanced Credit Bureau Dispute:
         Documentation   106
      Revolving Credit: Billing Clarification 108
      Revolving Credit: Change of Billing
         Address   110

Sample Explanation   112
Cease Communication   114
APPENDIXES
    I. *Credit Bureau and FTC Addresses*   117
    II. *Cost of Consumer Credit Reports*   118
    III. *Fair Credit Reporting Act*   119
    IV. *Fair Debt Collection Practices*   130
    V. *Fair Credit Billing Act*   141
    VI. *Truth in Lending Act*   148
    VII. *Using a Lawyer*   166

Note to the Reader

The information presented in this book is intended as a general guide to assist consumers in improving their credit rating. As different consumers have different credit histories, results from employing the methods in this book may vary. Neither this nor any other book should be used as a substitute for professional legal advice.

INTRODUCTION

OVERVIEW OF CREDIT REPORTING

We all remember the schoolteacher's nagging warning about a "permanent record" that would haunt us in our pursuit of everything from jobs and college admissions to the afterlife. Well, it's true.

If the information age has given birth to a Big Brother, it's the credit reporting industry. Nearly every adult in America is tracked by three main corporations—TRW, TransUnion, and Equifax. If you count the overlapping efforts, the Big Three have more than 450 million files. These files are called credit reports.

Most people have never given a second thought to their credit records. The credit bureaus—the companies that compile and issue reports on individual credit worthiness—don't want anyone to think about or question them, and they've been very successful in avoiding public scrutiny as their industry has grown over the last two decades. Even though credit reporting has evolved into a multibillion-dollar business, there is little public or governmental oversight of the credit reporting system. No one should be surprised to learn that this unsupervised system is grossly erratic and unfair.

Credit reports are the lifeblood of our credit-driven economy. When you apply for a loan—for a credit card, a mortgage, a car, or college—or sometimes even for job or insurance, someone is going to check your credit report. A credit report can clear or disqualify your application or, more insidiously, determine the terms of acceptance, such as the interest rate on a loan (higher and more expensive for someone with a spotty report). Every working day, about 1.5 million credit reports are issued, pronouncing citizens creditworthy or not.

The detail and scope of information in the bureaus' computer credit reports can be shockingly personal, sometimes including grooming habits and demeanor. And they are surprisingly public.

Virtually anyone who wants your report can get it. More ominous still, credit reports are often filled with mistakes. In a 1991 study, *Consumer Reports* estimated that half of all credit reports have errors. It's common, for instance, for the credit bureaus to confuse the separate credit histories of two people with the same name.

The credit reporting system can be confusing and intimidating, especially for people who have gotten into credit trouble. No creditor can push you around or harass you once you've read our book. Following simple instructions, you can manage what the credit bureaus say about you. This book won't get you out of your debts, but it will change the way they are reported.

HOW DOES THIS BOOK WORK?

Even if your credit is good, so much is riding on your credit history that it's in your interest to regularly check your credit report and clear any mistakes or other damaging information.

The book is organized into the three main steps to clean credit:

• Get Your Credit Report
• Read Your Credit Report
• Repair Your Credit Report

Each section has **basic** and **advanced** approaches depending on your interest and need.

You can set the repair process in motion today by sending away to the three main credit bureaus for copies of your credit reports. If you already know what your bad accounts are (a credit card, a car loan, etc.), you can begin fighting them immediately.

HOW DOES CREDIT REPAIR WORK?

This book raises a question: Can the average citizen really change what credit bureaus report? The answer is yes.

HOW CREDIT REPAIR WORKS

The secret of **basic** credit repair has a simple logic. Even though they may act like it, credit bureaus are not God or government.

Under current law, their right to mind other people's business—to sell information about you—comes with the responsibility to substantiate the information if it's challenged.

Credit repair is the process of persistently challenging the credit bureaus to document their information. The credit bureaus are expert at ignoring these challenges for technical reasons, but the system ultimately favors the persistent consumer who navigates the labyrinthine process. Why? Because, incredibly, the credit bureaus and creditors are so sloppy at verifying their information that they often prefer to restore your credit rather than to prove that it's bad. *When you exercise your rights, you turn the unfairness of the credit reporting system against itself.* The credit bureaus convict without proof, but when pressed, they also exonerate without proof. Credit bureaus would rather shut up than put up. Credit repair forces the bureaus to make this choice.

Sometimes the credit bureaus aren't the source of the problem. Creditors, who report to the credit bureaus, can be negotiated with and convinced to stop saying bad things about you. The **advanced** section walks you through creditor negotiations. Although most lenders value your patronage, the firm exercise of your rights under consumer laws is what usually persuades the creditor to clear your name.

THE CREDIT REPAIR INDUSTRY

There's an extensive cottage industry of paraprofessionals who make a living using many of the techniques in this book. This book is the most complete guide to proven credit repair techniques ever published.

Credit repair is a new field and, consequently, operates at the fringes of other businesses. You've probably seen ads on late-night television for credit repair services. Its practitioners, known as credit doctors, work behind the scenes with mortgage brokers, real-estate agents, financial planners, and lawyers. The size of the industry is difficult to measure in part because the best credit repair efforts are, by design, invisible to the credit bureaus. It's safe to say, though, that there are hundreds of people processing tens of thousands of disputes throughout the country every year.

Partly because the business is so young, and partly because its customers are often desperate, the credit repair industry has more than its fair share of quacks. One of the standard ruses is charging through a 900 line for stale repair information that merely fronts for a secured credit-card offer. There have been so many complaints of unfulfilled promises and outright consumer rip-offs that California and Florida now regulate credit repair. We hope that our book will empower consumers at a fraction of the upwards of $500 that credit repair services often charge, and that it will also teach people how to identify the crooked repair offers.

Even with our book, there's still a place for the experienced credit repair practitioner, especially in the areas of creditor negotiation and legal issues like filing court motions.

Part of being educated about what you can do is knowing what you can't. *The Guerrilla Guide* also teaches how to find and use a lawyer. Even then, this book is essential reading for working with a credit counselor or lawyer.

GET YOUR CREDIT REPORT

INTRODUCTION

Getting your credit reports is the first step to challenging their contents. Consequently, the credit bureaus don't make this any easier than they have to. By the logic of the credit bureaus, they're in business to sell credit histories, not to give them out for free.

Only recently and only under the threat of new federal regulation have they begun to acknowledge in their policies that people are entitled to review their own credit reports. Even with the new credit report glasnost, other people have a much easier time checking your own reports than you do. You, for example, have to send in documentation to get your report, then wait weeks for it to come; any credit professional can get the report faxed in minutes on the slightest pretense and with nothing more than your social security number or even your street address from the phone book.

There are three central credit bureaus that collect and resell the information in credit reports. These companies—TRW, TransUnion, and Equifax—repackage their files through their subsidiaries and hundreds of other data subcontractors. If you know what the three "super-bureaus" are saying about you, then you know everything about your credit, save what the corner grocer says.

GETTING PROFESSIONAL CREDIT REPORTS

The consumer version of the credit report, which you will get using the following steps, is sometimes less complete than the professional version used when someone checks your credit. To learn how to obtain the professional report on yourself, see **Advanced: Infiles** (page 18).

If you are applying for a mortgage, you should read the advanced discussion of mortgage reports, which are also different from consumer reports, in **Advanced: Full Factual and Residential Mortgage Credit Reports** (page 19).

STEPS

1. Determine if you have to pay for the reports. Personal files should be free for review to the people they are kept on, but they are often not. Special conditions:
   - Have you recently been rejected for a loan? If this is the case, you will use the "Requesting Your Free Report If You Were Denied Credit" letter (page 16). The law guarantees a free copy of any report that was used to deny you credit within the last 30 days.
   - As this edition goes to press, TRW offers one free report a year. TransUnion and Equifax do not, although they may also begin offering free reports on a limited basis in order to head off new industry regulations. For more, see the "Requesting Your Free Credit Report" letter (page 14).

2. Copy out a version of Form Letter 1 three times, once for *each of the companies*. The companies keep separate files, and you should collect your files from all three. It is important to:
   - include your Social Security number;
   - always use your present address, even if you have moved (the spelling of your name and your Social Security number are the two crucial pieces of information for retrieving credit reports);
   - verify your identity; to do this (and to hassle you), the credit bureaus often require you to enclose a photocopy of a utility bill, credit-card bill, or driver's license with your present address as above (you can use documentation that shows an older address if you identify it as a former address when specifying your present address);
   - sign and date the letter.
   If you've changed your name (through marriage, for example), you should make note of this whenever identifying yourself to the credit bureaus.

3. Address the envelopes. Credit bureau addresses are in Appendix I (page 117).

4. Protect yourself when you send these letters, and all other letters in this book, by:
   - using *certified/return receipt* mail. It's an excellent way to prove that you sent a letter. As this goes to press, the cost at the post office is $2.29. You don't need registered mail, which costs two dollars more;
   - keeping at least one photocopy of all correspondence you send to anyone.

5. Make a note of the day you sent off the report requests so you can follow up if necessary.

6. What if the credit report doesn't come within four weeks? Mark an extra photocopy of the original credit report request with your own version of the comment:

   ATTENTION FTC:
   It's been four weeks since I sent this letter certified/ return receipt, and my credit report has not come yet!

   Send this marked-up letter to the FTC (see Appendix I for address), and send a photocopy to the credit bureau. Don't forget: Send all correspondence *certified/return receipt*, and keep photocopies for your own records.

"Buying Your Credit Report" Letter

You should request the credit report from each of the three super-bureaus. Use this letter for credit bureaus that charge for their reports (at press, TransUnion and Equifax). Use "Requesting Your Free or Complimentary Credit Report" Letter for TRW.

The credit bureau addresses and report costs are found in Appendix I. You will probably want to pay by money order; the credit bureaus add on extra weeks to the delivery time waiting for a check to clear.

Remember when using this letter, and all letters in this book, to:

1. Reword the letter in your own words. You don't want to appear like you are being coached or following a repair strategy.
2. Keep a photocopy of the letter for your records. The copies are often used later in the repair process.
3. Send the letter through *certified/return receipt* mail. This is proof that you sent the letter.

credit bureau address

date

To Customer Service:

Enclosed in my money order for *cost of credit report* plus local sales tax. Please send my credit report to the following address:

your full name (include middle initial and any jr. or sr.)
your address here

[Include:]
your Social Security number
your year of birth

You will also find enclosed *documentation* verifying my identity. Thank you for your cooperation.

Sincerely,
your signature

"Requesting Your Free Credit Report" Letter

At press time, TRW is the only credit bureau that will send a consumer's report to the consumer without charge. The policy is limited to one report annually.

If you're not in a hurry and you want to save a few bucks, you can try sending a version of this letter to the credit bureaus that charge for reports and see what happens (maybe take out the word "complimentary"). The bureaus will sometimes send you a free report.

Remember when using this letter, and all letters in this book, to:

1. Reword the letter in your own words. You don't want to appear like you are being coached or following a repair strategy.
2. Keep a photocopy of the letter for your records. The copies are often used later in the repair process.
3. Send the letter through *certified/return receipt* mail. This is proof that you sent the letter.

credit bureau address

date

To Customer Service:

I am writing to request my complimentary report. Please send my credit report to the following address:

your full name (include middle initial and any jr. or sr.)
your address here

[Include:]
your Social Security number
your year of birth

You will also find enclosed *documentation* verifying my identity. Thank you for your cooperation.

Sincerely,
your signature

"Requesting Your Free Report If You Were Denied Credit" Letter

Use this letter if a credit report was used in a recent decision to deny you credit, insurance, or a job. Under law the credit bureau that issued the report is required to give you a free copy of your report if you request it within 30 days of being turned down (although, by company policy, TRW extends the time limit to 60 days).

How do you know if a credit report was used? The institution that turned you down is required to tell you if your credit history was reviewed, and also which credit bureau issued the report, although they are not required to provide you with a copy of the credit report.

Remember when using this letter, and all letters in this book, to:

1. Reword the letter in your own words. You don't want to appear like you are being coached or following a repair strategy.
2. Keep a photocopy of the letter for your records. The copies are often used later on in the repair process.
3. Send the letter through *certified/return receipt* mail. This is proof that you sent the letter.

credit bureau address

date

To Customer Service:

I was recently rejected for a *loan, job, or insurance policy* by *name of rejector* on *date of rejection*. The decision included use of a credit report from your service. I would like a copy of my report so I can look into this matter. Please send my credit report to the following address:

your full name (include middle initial and any jr. or sr.)
your address here

[Include:]
your Social Security number
your year of birth

You will also find enclosed *documentation* verifying my identity. Thank you for your cooperation.

Sincerely,
your signature

ADVANCED: INFILES

INTRODUCTION

Not all credit reports are equal. The report that the credit bureaus will send you on yourself is often not as complete as the report they send lending professionals. The professional reports are known as "infiles." Derogatory information, especially the timing of any late payments, is difficult to read or omitted on TRW and Equifax consumer reports, but clearly summarized in the professional infiles. In addition, TRW gives a national risk score of your overall credit worthiness (between 0 and 1000, with 0 the best credit) that they conveniently leave off the consumer version. TransUnion gets high marks for their consumer reports, which are just as complete and well organized as the professional version.

Companies that subscribe to the credit bureaus or the credit-bureau subsidiaries are prohibited by their agreements with the credit bureaus from giving consumers a copy of their own infile. The credit bureaus claim this is to prevent fraud, but it seems more likely that the credit bureaus just don't want consumers to see what the lending professionals see when they look into your life.

There are laws that make it a criminal offense to access credit records for purposes other than judging whether or not an individual with whom you are contemplating a business transaction is creditworthy. Still, it's simple for any private detective, landlord, or employer to get your infile by supplying your name and Social Security number to a credit service. And just think how often you give out your Social Security number.

If you can get them, infiles are not only more complete, they are also usually faster to buy. An infile can be faxed to you on the same day you order it.

GETTING INFILES

One quick way to get infiles is to register yourself as a prospective landlord or employer with a local credit bureau. Registration is often shockingly simple, considering the privacy questions involved. You can usually register the same day you call if you have a fax machine.

Once you have registered, you can have credit reports sent

by fax or mail to you within hours. (Consumers wait weeks for their reports after ordering them.) Credit bureaus can sometimes pull a file with nothing more than a name and street address, but the Social Security number is always helpful. Infiles can range in price from $2.75 for regular customers to between $8 and $15 for infrequent customers. Profiteers sell them for as much as $25 or even $50, ordering your report for you and then charging a mark-up for the service.

Local credit bureaus are usually listed in the yellow pages of metropolitan areas under "credit." If you can't find one, ask a mortgage or other lending professional which bureau his or her company uses. Because you can't order your own report, someone else has to be the prospective landlord or employer to pull your file.

ADVANCED: FULL FACTUAL AND RESIDENTIAL MORTGAGE CREDIT REPORTS

The credit reports used in evaluating mortgage applications are special. You don't ever hold it in your hands, but you usually pay for it and you should know what it contains. As part of the application process, the mortgage broker will send you a form asking you to explain any bad credit that appears in the report.

A **full factual** or residential report, as they are also called, is a combination of two infiles. The rules for mortgage applications warrant that two infiles be combined as the basis for deciding your creditworthiness. TRW and TransUnion infiles are a common combination, and some companies combine these two and Equifax. Depending on where you live, any combination is possible.

In effect, you can get your full factual by getting the infiles that will be used for it (see **Infiles**, above). Ask your mortgage broker, should you be in the process of applying, which bureaus are used for the full factual reports that the broker orders. This will allow you to focus your credit disputes on the sources of your credit reports for your mortgage application.

Full factual reports are more expensive than infiles or consumer reports, often costing $50. For this fee, a credit-bureau employee will check on the consumer with calls to employers, landlords, present mortgage providers, and any creditors commented on or disputed in the mortgage application.

(For the last reason above, if you are disputing items on your credit report in an effort to have them removed—and the creditors disagree with your position—it is not in your interest to bring these items up on your mortgage application. You are much better off dealing directly with the credit bureaus or creditors as detailed in the **repair** section.)

The full factual service can sometimes accelerate credit repair efforts (see **Advanced Repair: Full Factual Glossing**).

READ YOUR CREDIT REPORT

INTRODUCTION

Credit reports are usually difficult to read because most weren't originally designed for consumers, and because the credit bureaus know that you're less likely to dispute what you can't understand.

If reading a credit report is unfamiliar to you, follow the step-by-step guide that follows. The reading section only focuses on identifying what's bad on your reports and the information you'll need for planning your repair effort. The **Advanced Repair** section covers the multitude of details that makes the reports so confusing, although the information will only prove useful in unusual cases.

There are many different styles of credit report, but they all derive from the one of the three super-bureaus that supplied the information being reported. The instructions for reading your credit report are different for each of the three credit bureaus. Regional credit bureaus, which resell reports from the three major credit bureaus, often use their own formats. The regional reports contain the same information, but you'll have to work a little harder to find it on the page. Nevertheless, the explanations in this section still apply. They are organized around identifying the basic information you need for repairing bad credit:

- creditor name (and type of creditor)
- account number
- status
- lateness patterns

We recommend using a colored highlighter to mark up your report as you decipher it.

Some of the information, such as your name and address, may not be new to you, but it's useful to know what the credit bureau has listed anyway. Tiny mistakes in any of the most mundane information can affect your credit rating, especially if it means you have been confused with someone else with a similar name.

HELP FROM THE CREDIT BUREAUS

The flipside of most credit reports contains some information that you should read through. The credit bureaus also publish materials to help you read your credit report. You may find them useful. The TRW Consumer Credit Services pamphlet is called *Understanding TRW's Credit Reporting Service*. TransUnion and Equifax each publish annotated guides to the reports.

As this book goes to press, the credit bureau materials tend to deemphasize harmful information in their explanations. Not surprisingly, they tend to dissuade challenges to the reporting system by suggesting ineffective dispute resolution methods such as adding a consumer statement to explain a harmful item. In order to head off legislative reform of the reporting system, the credit bureaus may improve the readability of the credit reports. TRW, for instance, has begun printing some of their consumer reports in plain English.

Identifying Derogatory Items on a TRW Consumer Credit Report

TRW CONSUMER CREDIT REPORT

If you request your free annual report from TRW, you will get this version of your credit history.

Its advantage is the plain language that it is written in. On some—but not all—reports, derogatory items are identified with an asterisk ("*") to the left of the creditor name, and in the right-hand Status/Payments column.

The disadvantage of the Consumer Credit Report is that it leaves out valuable information for assessing your credit rating and challenging harmful elements of it. The bottom line is that you have to work harder to dispute items from a Consumer Credit Report. Specifically: There is no 24-month history of payments, which is included on the professional version. Without this, there is no way for you to know when delinquencies were reported. You will have to get this information from the creditor. Some of these reports even omit the asterisk ("*") that identifies harmful information on the professional versions.

Identifying Derogatory Items on a TRW Updated Credit Profile Disclosure Report

TRW UPDATED CREDIT PROFILE DISCLOSURE

A sample TRW Updated Credit Profile Disclosure appears on page 26. You'll end up with this version of your TRW credit report in response to a written dispute of bad credit items that you've sent TRW. It usually is not complete, only listing items that you've disputed.

Each creditor is listed horizontally across the Credit Profile. The creditor's reports are the meat of your credit history. The following categories of information apply to each creditor.

POS I NON I NEG

The left-hand side of the Credit Profile has three columns:

Pos   Non   Neg

Each credit item is assigned to one column, and designated with a letter. (The letter refers to the manner in which the information was verified, but this is not important for credit repair.)

If the particular item is "positive," it's good credit.

If it's "negative," it's hurting your credit rating.

If it's "non," it's likely to be bad credit. This ostensibly neutral rating is usually applied to items that were at some point late or delinquent but are now up-to-date or paid. This is still a mark against you. For example, several "non"-rated credit cards would probably disqualify you for a mortgage. Overdue reform of the credit reporting system should address the misleading representation of bad credit to the consumer as neutral.

IDENTIFYING THE CREDITOR (OR PUBLIC RECORD)

The name of the creditor is found to the right of the "Pos I Non I Neg" columns. There are many pieces of information about the account, but at this stage you only want this.

Updated CREDIT PROFILE SM
Report

TRW

Inquiry Information

TCR2 6102 3499953
Anytown, USA 12345, L-80

Public, Jay Q . ...,176 8 11432,Z–ME, S– 543224414,123 Easy Street,

IDENTIFICATION NUMBER

NE 0	PAGE 1	DATE 04/10/92	TIME 3:51:54	PORT	H/V		TNJ1	56-255264/56

Account Profile			Subscriber Name/Court Name			Subscriber # Court Code	Assn. Code	Amount			Account/Docket Number		Payment Profile number of months prior to balance date
Pos.	Non.	Neg.	Status Comment	Status Date	Date Opened	Type	TER MS			Balance	Balance Date	Amount Past Due	1 2 3 4 5 6 7 8 9 10 11 12
A			MANUF HANOVER PAID SATIS	12-91	12-87	1101000 BUS	1 41	ORIGL $4,0000	$0		123456789123 12-31-91		
		⟶	ITEM CHANGED AS ABOVE										
	A		SAKS FIFTH AVENUE CURWAS30+6	11-90	10-Y	1347515 CHG SCH	1 REV MONTH PAY	HIBAL $3000 $213	$2139		12345678 1-23-92 LAST PAY 01-18-92		
		⟶	ABOVE ITEM REMAINS - CONFIRMED BY SOURCE										
	A		NEW YORK CNTY REG JUDGMT SAT	10-18-90		1011035		$400			00000001 NYC DEPT FINANCE		
		⟶	ABOVE ITEM REMAINS - CONFIRMED BY SOURCE										
			B ALTMAN & CO.				ACCOUNT # UNKNOWN						
		⟶	ITEM NO LONGER APPEARS ON YOUR REPORT										
			FIRST CARD				ACCOUNT # 123456789						
		⟶	ITEM NO LONGER APPEARS ON YOUR REPORT										
		⟶	END										

This report is based on the identifying information supplied by you. If you did not supply us with your full name, addresses for the past 5 years, social security number and year of birth, this report may not be complete.

IDENTIFYING THE ACCOUNT NUMBER

The account number is essential for all communications with creditors and credit bureaus. This is found in the column running down the right-side of the report. Make a note of it or mark it. (Sometimes account numbers are truncated to limit fraud, usually with credit cards.)

READING THE ACCOUNT STATUS TERMS

Account status is found directly under the creditor name. The status lines explain in detail the actual meaning of the "Pos I Non I Neg" ratings. The status data determines your credit rating.

Sometimes a 24-month account history (coded on two lines—typically something like "CCCCCCCCCCC1") will appear along with the account number on the right-hand side. If it does, see **24-Month Account History** in the **Infile** write-up (page 31). In the sample credit report here, it is omitted.

Status Terms for Good Credit

CURR ACCT This is a good and open account.
PAID ACCT This is a closed, good account, now fully paid.
PAID SATIS Also a closed, good account.

These above are the only acceptable ratings on a credit account. Almost all other ratings hurt you, excepting some that reflect procedural issues in the handling of your accounts such as transfers. Therefore, as you set about the process of disputing your credit, look suspiciously at any credit settlement that doesn't change the account status to one of the three listed above.

"Current" Status Terms for Bad Credit

The following "Current" accounts usually result in a "Non" rating even though the account is up-to-date as of the creditor's last report. Don't be misled; it's still harmful to your credit rating.

CUR WAS 30 An account that's presently on time but was 30 days late at least once in the last 7 years. Variations are CUR WAS 60, 90, 120, 150, 180.
CUR WAS 30-2 This means that the account was 30 days late at least two times. Often an account with repeated 30's is only listed

as CUR WAS 30. The addition of the 30-2 often comes after a continuing pattern of double 30-day lates.

(Many accounts listed simply as WAS 30 actually had a number of 30-day lates and the reporting creditor used its discretion to give the consumer some slack.)

CUR WAS COL This is a current account that was in collection at some point in the past seven years.

CUR WAS DL A current account that was delinquent. "Delinquent" means not only was payment late but collection efforts were made.

CUR WAS FOR A current account that was in foreclosure.

CR LN CLOS An account that has been closed. These closures are often requested by consumers, but no matter who requests the account be closed, this status often includes the additional phrase "subscriber request," which means that your creditor (the one who "subscribes" to the credit bureau) requested the line be closed. Though it is not expressly described as a derogatory credit status, it is often considered bad credit. You have to know it's bad to fight it.

"Delinquent" Status Terms for Bad Credit
All "Delinquent" accounts result in a "Neg" rating.

DELINQ 60 This account is now 60 days delinquent. Variations include DELINQ 90, 120, 150, 180.

DEL WAS 90 This account was 90 days delinquent and is now 60 days delinquent.

DEL WAS 120 This account was 120 days delinquent, now 90, 60, or 30 days delinquent.

GOV CLAIM This is a claim for the insured part of a defaulted student loan.

"Charge Off" Status Terms for Bad Credit
All "Charge-Off" accounts result in a "Neg" rating.

CHARGE OFF This is an account that is written off as a loss for tax purposes by the creditor. A charge off can be for an extremely low amount of money, but no matter how small, it is severely damaging to your credit. It is notable that the creditors make money by charging off the "losses," because they lower the amount of taxable income the creditor needs to declare. Even if you weren't properly notified that the charge existed, they will call it a loss. Many charge-offs come from additional account charges, accounts with only a few dollars owing, or annual fees that accrue whether you know it or not. When you fail to pay, they charge it off, usually automatically, when tax time comes. They win small, you lose big.

PD CHARGE OFF, This is a charge-off that you've paid. Even though the debt is settled, this credit status is almost as bad as a charge-off.

IDENTIFYING THE STATUS DATE

The status date refers to the last time the item was reported to the credit bureau. The age of an item can help plan repair strategy.

If the date is current within the last three months, that means that the creditor most likely keeps your account in its current files.

If the status date is more than a year old, the creditor has probably shifted the records of your account to its archives. Archival accounts are less likely to be verified when challenged.

Identifying Derogatory Items on a TRW Infile

TRW INFILE

A sample TRW Infile appears on page 30. The infile version of your TRW credit history is sent to potential lenders who want to check your credit history. It is a complete credit history, as opposed to the usually sanitized TRW Consumer Credit Report, or Updated Credit Profile.

To read your infile, follow the instructions for decoding the TRW Updated Credit Profile Disclosure (referred to as Credit Profile). Keep in mind the following differences:

ASTERISK ("*") COLUMN

Unlike the Credit Profile, there are no misleading "Pos | Non | Neg" ratings. All harmful credit items are marked with an "*" in the far left-hand column, adjacent to the creditor's name.

IDENTIFYING THE CREDITOR (OR PUBLIC RECORD)

The name of the creditor is found at the left-margin, in a similar position as on the Credit Profile.

TRW Infile

```
TNJ1
ADS  1908491  Public J. Q. . . . . , 176 8 11432,
S-123456789  Y-1931,H-Y,

PAGE 1  DATE  2-11-92  TIME  9:29:57  PCY06  V302  TNJ1

Jay Q. Public              SSN: 123 45 6789        EMPL: Any Company USA
123 Easy St.               YOB: 1960               RPTD: 8-88
Anytown, USA 12345         SPOUSE: S
RPTD: 12-91U
```

PROFILE SUMMARY:

PUBLIC RECORDS	1	PAST DUE AMT	$0	INQUIRIES	1	SATIS ACCTS	35
INSTALL BAL	$12,155	SCH/EST PAY	$2,993*	INQS/6 MON	0	NOW DEL/DRG	0
R ESTATE BAL	N/A	R ESTATE PAY	N/A	TRADELINES	40	WAS DEL/DRG	4
REVOLVING BAL	$217,656	REVOLVNG AVAIL	16%*	PAID ACCTS	10	OLD TRADE	10-Y

```
NATIONAL RISK SCORE = 12     SCORE FACTORS: J, A, I, E.


  PUBLIC RECORDS:
*NEW YORK CNTY REG      10-18-90    1011035    $400      JUDGMT SAT
 CASE: 00000001      PLAINTIFF: NYC DEPT FINANCE
```

SUBSCRIBER ACCOUNT # SUBSCR #	TYPE	TERMS	ECOA	DATE OPN BAL DATE LAST PAY	AMT/TYPE BALANCE MONTH PAY	STATUS DATE $PASTDUE	ACCT STATUS PYMT HISTORY IN PRIOR MOS
CITIBANK NA QUEENS 82364149 1100772	C/C	REV	1	2-83 11-29-91 11-91	$19,500 L $11,500	11-91	CURR ACCT CCCCCCCCCCCCC CCCCCCCCCCCCC
*MANUF HANOVER 670461456051 1101000	BUS	41	1	12-87 12-31-91	$40,000 O $0	12-91	PD WAS 60 -222221-CCCC 1CCCCCCCCCCCC
EURO-AM BK 595360488 1102842	C/C	REV	1	10-Y 1-31-92 12-91	$7,000 $0	1-92	CURR ACCT NNNNNNNNNNNN NNNNNNNNNNNN
NATL WESTMINSTER BANK 7102533268 1103100	C/C	60	4	10-Y 12-31-91 12-91	$15,000 L $5,236	12-91	CURR ACCT CCCCC-CCCCCC CCCCCCCCCCCCC
V N B 530000150065	BUS	10	1	9-87 7-12-91	$22,500 O $10,000	7-91	CURR ACCT

IDENTIFYING THE ACCOUNT NUMBER

This number is found just below the creditor name, and is not to be confused with the subscriber number located just below the account number. Subscriber numbers are usually shorter, except in cases when credit card account numbers are truncated to limit fraud:

> EURO-AM BK
> 59536 *This is the truncated account number.*
> 1102842 *This subscriber number identifies the creditor to the credit bureau.*

READING THE ACCOUNT STATUS TERMS

Account status is found at the far-right of the page. The terms are the same as on the Credit Profile, but the infile also lists the 24-month account history (coded on two lines—typically something like "CCCCCCCCCCC1") underneath the status term (see below).

24-MONTH ACCOUNT HISTORY

A typical entry looks like this:

> CUR WAS 30-3
> CCCCCCCCCCC1
> 11CCNNNCCCCC

The first line is the status term (see **Reading the Account Status Terms**, above).

The position of the letters and numbers represent the last 24 months, with the upper-left being the month of the status date (most recent). Reading across on the top line, the top right is the twelfth most recent month, and, reading across on the bottom line, the bottom-right is the oldest month.

The Meanings of the Letter and Number Symbols
"C" Current Account. Payment was on-time.
"N" Current Account. There is a zero balance—no money owed.
"1" Payment was 30 days late. (On some reports, however, "1" is used to represent an on-time payment. You can identify this situation if the status term of an account with lots of 1's reads "Cur." In this case, the

following numbers refer to late payments shifted one-month less. For example, "2" would refer to a payment that was 30 days late.) Under most circumstances, the following meanings apply:

"2"   Payment was 60 days late.
"3"   Payment was 90 days late.
"4"   Payment was 120 days late.
"5"   Payment was 150 days late.
"6"   Payment was 180 days late.
"-"   No history report.
blank   No history maintained.

IDENTIFYING THE STATUS DATE

On an infile, there are a number of dates, most of which are not important to the repair process. The status date is important. Located just to the left of the account status section on the most right column, the status date indicates the last time they updated your file to include account status terms such as CUR WAS 30. The status date is important for determining how to dispute an item. A status date older than a year indicates that an account is likely no longer active. Records for accounts with these older status dates may be kept in archives, and this is a boon to anyone who is disputing bad credit. Creditors are often loathe to look up archival information, and some make it a policy to ignore disputes on old paid accounts.

Even if the status date is for the most recent month, this does not mean that your bad credit results from that month. The account status section, especially the 24-month history, gives you the best idea of when your bad credit marks were added to the file. The status date helps you interpret the 24-month history, because it represents the top-left account month on the 24-month section, thus allowing you to count back and know exactly which month is being called late.

Identifying Derogatory Items on a Transunion Consumer Relations Disclosure and Infile

TRANSUNION CONSUMER RELATIONS DISCLOSURE AND INFILE

A sample Transunion Consumer Relations Disclosure appears on page 34. Transunion sends the Consumer Relations Disclosure to consumers and infiles to lending professionals. They are essentially the same.

Each creditor is listed horizontally across the Credit Profile. The creditors' reports are the meat of your credit history. Apply the following explanations to one creditor at a time.

IDENTIFYING THE CREDITOR (OR PUBLIC RECORD)

The name of the creditor is found at the left margin. There are many pieces of information about the account, but at this stage you only want this.

IDENTIFYING THE ACCOUNT NUMBER

This number is found just below the creditor name, not to be confused with the subscriber number located just to the right of the creditor name. (Subscriber numbers often have a letter as the first digit, and they are usually shorter than the account number. Account numbers can be shorter if they are for credit card accounts—credit card account numbers are truncated to limit fraud.)

> CHASE MAN BK B 402D010 *This subscriber number identifies the creditor to the credit bureau.*
>
> 3890193 *This is the truncated account number.*

READING THE ACCOUNT STATUS TERMS

Found at the far-right of the page with the heading "Type of Account & MOP [method of payment]." The first account status rating is a letter "I," "R," "C," or "O" followed by a number from 01 to 09. "I" refers to installment credit; "R" refers to revolving credit; "C" refers to a line of credit on your checking account; and

TRANS UNION
CONSUMER RELATIONS DISCLOSURE
NOT TO BE USED AS A CREDIT REPORT

DEAR CONSUMER:
THIS IS A COPY OF THE CURRENT CONTENTS OF YOUR FILE IT IS BEING FURNISHED TO YOU BASED ON THE INFORMATION YOU HAVE PROVIDED IN ACCORDANCE WITH THE "FAIR CREDIT REPORTING ACT" PLEASE PROVIDE THE FILE NUMBER SHOWN ON THIS REPORT ON ALL CORRESPONDENCE REFER TO THE REVERSE SIDE FOR EXPLANATIONS OF CODES AND ABBREVIATIONS IN THIS DISCLOSURE.

FILE NUMBER		
93AA0000-000	03	CC
DATE		
07/09/92	INDIVIDUAL	NY
AMOUNT RECIEVED	PAYMENT TYPE	
CREDIT CARD NO.		EXP. DATE

IN FILE SINCE   09/55

BIRTH DATE   6/60

CONSUMER NAME AND ADDRESS	SSN	DATE RPTD
02/92	123-45-6789	
	SPOUSE NAME SSN	

Public, Jay Q.
123 Easy Street
Anytown, USA 12345

TEL   555-2045

DATE REPORTED
04/93

FORMER ADDRESS

PRESENT EMPLOYER AND ADDRESS   POSITION INCOME   EMPL DATE   DATE VERIF

FORMER EMPLOYER AND ADDRESS

SPOUSE'S EMPLOYER AND ADDRESS

SUBSCRIBER NAME	SUBSCRIBER CODE	DATE OPENED	HIGH CREDIT	DATE VERIFIED	BALANCE OWING	AMOUNT PAST DUE	PAYMENT PATTERN 1-12 MONTHS 13-24 MONTHS	TYPE ACCOUNT & MOP
ECDA ACCOUNT NUMBER COLLATERAL	TERMS		CREDIT LIMIT	DATE CLOSED REMARKS	DATE	AMOUNT	MOP HISTORICAL STATUS NO. OF MONTHS 30-59 60-89 90+	
SAKS 5TH AVE C 2163001	7/72	$3093	7/92V	$1464	$0	11XXXXXXX111 1111221111X1 47 7 0 0	RO1
13885744 I							
MBUSA/MACY'S D 235002S	7/59	$2050	6/92A	$874	$0	111111122211 111111111111 48 3 0 0	RO1
24874533 I BRCL3B DL1487		$0					
LORD & TAYLOR D 1643001	1/57	$1303	8/89A			111111211111 1111 16 1 0 0	RO1
33208314 C							
AMERICAN EXP N 656N001	9/75	$288	6/92A	$288	$0	1111111111X1 XX111X111111 33 0 0 0	OO1
4728101877 I							
GECAP / LEVITZ Q 2350440	7/89	$660	6/92A	$307	$0	111111111111 1111XXXXXXXX 38 0 0 0	RO1
63435902 P BRCC7A DL4343							
CHASE MAN BK B 402D010	10/88		6/92A	$4249	$0	11111111X111 1X11X1X1X11X 12 0 0 0	RO1
3595187 I	MIN88	$4500					
CHASE MAN BK B 402D010	7/79	$0	6/92A	$3106	$0	111111111121 111132111111 12 0 0 0	RO1
3890193 I	MIN64	$3400					
AMERICAN EXP N 656N002	9/75	$151	6/92A	$2735	$0	1111111111X1 XX1XXXXXXXXX 48 0 0 0	RO1
2728101877 I							

INQUIRY

DATE	ECOA	SUBCODE	SUBNAME	TYPE AMT
04/03/92	I	Z OH5251	CONSUM DISCL	

N 0012267-12/28/91 - I , N 0004790-03/02/91-I, N 1212137-11/21/90 - I

"O" refers to an open account with relaxed payment deadlines. A "09" is the worst credit, usually reserved for charge-offs. A typical rating "R01" refers to a current account, but it can still mask a harmful credit mark in the payment history (see below). You can be sure that anything but "01" rating is bad credit.

The second account status rating is a payment history, typically composed of a two-line 24-month history and a "Historical Status" line of four numbers that summarize late payments:

111111111121   *24-Month History*
11113211111
        48 2 1 0   *Historical Status*

READING THE 24-MONTH HISTORY

The position of the numbers represent the last 24 months, with the upper-left being the month of the status date (most recent). Reading across on the top line, the top-right is the twelfth most recent month; reading across on the bottom line, the bottom-right is the oldest month.

The Meanings of the Numbers
"1"   Payment was on-time.
"2"   Payment was 30 days late.
"3"   Payment was 60 days late.
"4"   Payment was 90 days late.
"5"   Payment was 120 days late.
"6"   Payment was 150 days late.
"7"   Payment was 180 days late.
"X"   No history report.
blank   No history maintained.

The Historical Status (line of four numbers) explained. Reading from left to right, the numbers refer to:

- how many months back the credit records go (48 here)
- the number of payments reported as 30 days late (2 here)
- the number of payments reported as 60 days late (1 here)
- the number of payments reported as 90 days (or more) late (none here)

Because credit records can be reported for seven years or more, it's possible to see a clean 24-month history that still shows "lates" in the Historical Status section.

IDENTIFYING THE "DATE VERIFIED"

The "Date Verified" column reveals how recently your credit was reported from a particular creditor. If the Date Verified is more than a year old, the account is probably not active anymore.

Because creditors and credit bureaus usually report bad credit for many years (seven years in most cases), it's possible to see a recently verified bad-credit mark on an account that has been current for some time. This is a source of confusion to many consumers, who wonder why an account that has been paid well for years can still register as a recent report of bad credit.

The "Date Verified" also identifies the date of the top-left month in the 24-month history. With this information, you can count back and determine the exact date of bad-credit marks in the 24-month history.

Identifying Derogatory Items on an Equifax Credit History

EQUIFAX CREDIT HISTORY

A sample Equifax Credit History appears on pages 38–9. Equifax sends the credit history reports to consumers and infiles to lending professionals. They are essentially the same in content, with slight variations in layout.

Each creditor is listed horizontally across the credit history. The creditors' reports are the meat of your credit history. Apply the following explanations to one creditor at a time.

IDENTIFYING THE CREDITOR (OR PUBLIC RECORD)

The first column, "Company Name," is found at the left margin. There are many pieces of information about the account, but at this stage you only want to identify the name of the creditor.

IDENTIFYING THE ACCOUNT NUMBER

This number is found in the second column from the left, "Account Number."

READING THE ACCOUNT STATUS TERMS

Account status is found in the second column from the right side of the page, "Status."

The first account status rating is a letter "I," "O," or "R" followed by a number from 1 to 9. "I" refers to installment credit; "O" refers to open credit with relaxed payment terms; "R" refers to revolving credit. A "9" is the worst credit, usually reserved for charge-offs. A typical rating "R1" refers to a current account, but it can still mask a harmful credit mark in the payment history (see below). You can be sure that anything but a "1" rating is bad credit.

PRIOR PAYING HISTORY

Any account that lists late payments will contain, underneath the creditor name, a line beginning ">>> PRIOR PAYING HISTORY" followed by a series of numbers and letters. Accounts that do not contain the prior paying message are clean.

The Prior Paying History follows a standard format, as demonstrated in decoding the following example:

>>> PRIOR PAYING HISTORY - 30(09)60(02)
90+(00)06/92-R2,04/92-R2,12/91-R3

The numbers in parentheses count the number of times the account was 30 days, 60 days, or more than 90 days late, reading from left to right. In this example, the account was paid 30 days late a total of nine times; 60 days, twice; and never 90 or more days late.

The dates following those numbers show changes in the account status, indicating approximately when the delinquencies occurred. The worst status rating, R3, was given to the account when the two 60-day lates were recorded in 12/91.

IDENTIFYING THE "DATE REPORTED"

The right-most, "Date Reported" column reveals how recently your credit was reported from a particular creditor. If the Date Reported is more than a year old, the account is probably not active anymore.

Because creditors and credit bureaus usually report bad credit for many years (seven years in most cases), it's possible to see a recently verified bad-credit mark on an account that has been

Jay Public
123 Easy Street
Anytown, USA 12345

*Please address all future
correspondence to this address* ➥

EQUIFAX CREDIT INFORMATION SERVICES
P O BOX 740256
ATLANTA, GA 30374

DATE 03/29/93
SOCIAL SECURITY NUMBER 123-45-6789
DATE OF BIRTH 06/11/60

CREDIT HISTORY

Company Name	Account Number	Whose Acct.	Date Opened	Months Re-viewed	Date Of Last Activity	High Credit	Terms	Items as of Date Reported			Date Reported
								Balance	Past Due	Status	
SAKS	857	I	07/72	99	02/92	3093	195	1953		R1	02/92
>>> PRIOR PAYING HISTORY – 30(09)60(02)90+(00)06/92-R2,04/92-R2,12/91-R3 <<<											
MBNA AMER	03159511	I	03/86	12	02/92	16K	379	15K		R1	02/92
AMOUNT IN H/C COLUMN IS CREDIT LIMIT											
AMEXTRVLSV	2929	I	06/75	49	03/92	3000		1419		R1	03/92
AMOUNT IN H/C COLUMN IS CREDIT LIMIT											
CITIBNK CC	82364149	I	02/83	99	01/92	19K		11K		R1	01/92
AMEXTRVLSV	9591987	I	05/75	48	02/92	0		0		R1	02/92
CLOSED ACCOUNT											
AMEXTRVLSV	59198	I	05/75	48	02/92	0		0		01	02/92
CLOSED ACCOUNT											

WALLACHS'S	1760	U	01/73	03	02/92	550	25	104	R1	03/92
CHASE-C R	1709	J	02/92		02/92	1500		0	R0	02/92
AMOUNT IN H/C COLUMN IS CREDIT LIMIT										
MBUSAMACYS	1487-4533	I	07/59	12	02/92	2050	99	992	R1	02/92
>>> PRIOR PAYING HISTORY – 3D(03)60(00)90+(00) <<<										
EAB OD	3604	I	06/79	53	12.91	7000		0	R1	02/92
LINE OF CREDIT										
CHASE (USA)	3890193	I	07/79	16	03/92	3400	62	2701	R1	02/92
AMOUNT IN H/C COLUMN IS CREDIT LIMIT										
DINER	7001727	I	05/79	29	02/92	620		0	01	02/92
AMEXTRVLSV	28101877	I	09/75	47	02/92	0		2216	R1	02/92

********* COURTHOUSE RECORDS **********

>>> JUDGEMENT FILED 04/90, MAN SUPRM, CASE NUMBER, DEFENDANT Jay Q Public
AMOUNT-$421, PLAINTIFF-NYC DEPT FINANCE

********** COMPANIES THAT REQUESTED YOUR CREDIT HISTORY *********

02/14/92 AR 404B800182
11/18/91 AR 458B800120

03/29/93 EQUIFAX
12/28/92 GECC
10/01/92 AR 444DC104?0

U93-RESTART 00041
****

COMPLETE PAGE 1 OF 1

current for some time. This is a source of confusion to many consumers, who wonder why an account that has been paid well for years can still register as a recent report of bad credit.

NOTE FOR EQUIFAX INFILE

Equifax infiles include a 24-month payment history that does not appear on the consumer's credit history. Use the TransUnion explanation (page 35) to decode the Equifax 24-month history if one appears on your report.

REPAIR YOUR CREDIT REPORT

INTRODUCTION: BASIC AND ADVANCED

By this point in the steps to repairing your credit rating, you have received and decoded your credit reports from the three major credit bureaus. You have identified the harmful information they are reporting on you, and you are ready to change it.

The repair process is divided into two sections. The first, **basic**, takes you through the process of written disputes with credit bureaus. The second, **advanced**, gives you a strategic perspective on the fastest and most effective dispute techniques for different combinations of bad credit. The techniques counseled in the **advanced** section include when to rely on the **basic** instructions, but also include creditor negotiation, full factual glossing, and use of the Fair Credit Reporting Act and Fair Credit Billing Act.

The **basic** disputes are straightforward and will work very well for the majority of derogatory credit items, but they are slow. At the minimum, disputes with the credit bureaus will take one to two months.

If you're not succeeding with the credit bureaus alone, or you want to plan the smartest, fastest, most effective course of action at the outset, make sure to also read the **advanced** section. The main focus of the **advanced** section is negotiating with creditors as opposed to the **basic** technique of challenging the credit bureaus.

BASIC CREDIT BUREAU DISPUTES

Most credit repair is done by disputing derogatory items with the three main credit bureaus. Even when more elaborate negotiations are needed with particular creditors, the credit bureaus are the ones that must ultimately clear your credit.

The simple secret to the techniques described in the section on basic credit bureau disputes, is: *The credit bureaus don't have the time or inclination to substantiate the validity of information they report when you challenge them.*

The laziness of the credit bureaus creates a bad system—imagine all the mistakes they make, not bothering to check the information that they resell!—but it's one that you can turn to your advantage. If you demand that the credit bureaus perform at the level implied by the appropriate regulation, they will often clear the record rather than spend time and resources picking over an individual issue. The system cannot ordinarily handle people who won't take no for an answer.

Step-by-Step Basic Credit Bureau Disputes

The steps that follow for disputing derogatory items with the three major credit bureaus are straightforward. They essentially involve sending a series of letters to each of the credit bureaus.

If you have three or fewer items to dispute, use the **Basic Dispute Flowchart for Disputing Three or Fewer Items** (on the next page); if you have more, use the **Basic Dispute Flowchart for Disputing Four or More Items** (page 49).

Often the credit bureaus will throw obstacles in your way. Here is exactly how not to take no for an answer, and to move step by step through a process that was designed by the credit bureaus to wear out your patience and make you quit.

If, at the end of the series of letters, you are not successful (unlikely in simple cases; likely in severe situations), go to the **advanced** section on creditor disputes.

There are five escalating letters in this **basic** section:

1. the initial dispute;
2. the second notice (to hurry response to initial dispute);
3. demand letter 1 (if no items are corrected);
4. demand letter 2 (if some items but not all are corrected);
5. the secondary dispute letter (after some success, to dispute more items).

The basic dispute process is organized around the letters. The instructions for executing each letter are included with a sample of each letter on the following pages. The letters are only useful if you trace your progress on the following **Basic Dispute**

Flowchart, because the timing of the letters is as important as what they say.

Basic Dispute Flowchart for Disputing Three or Fewer Items

You have to get your credit report from each of the credit bureaus, because they're separate reporting agencies, because they often report different things, and because you can't know which report someone is going to use to deny you credit. This means that you have to dispute similar items on different credit reports, credit bureau by credit bureau. Clearing an item on one bureau's report won't clear it off another—but, if you succeed in clearing an item off one report, it's an indication that you'll likely succeed with another credit bureau. When you have three or fewer items to dispute with each of the bureaus, you should conduct the disputes concurrently.

1. Send **initial dispute letter.**

2. Thirty days after Step 1, send **second-notice letter**. (This is almost always necessary, as credit bureaus rarely respond within 30 days. The Fair Credit Reporting Act requires credit bureaus to conclude their investigations "in a reasonable period of time." Courts have interpreted this to mean between 30 to 45 days. You can hold them to this.)

3. If, 10 days after Step 2, the credit bureaus still haven't responded, send the **FTC dispute letter** with a copy of your **second-notice letter** to both the FTC and the credit bureaus.

4. When you get a response from the credit bureaus, there are three possibilities:
   a. They remove *all* the derogatory items that you disputed. *You won!* The credit repair is complete.
      How to recognize this response from TRW. This will appear on a TRW "credit update" as "ABOVE ITEM DELETED" or "ITEM

Basic Dispute Flowchart

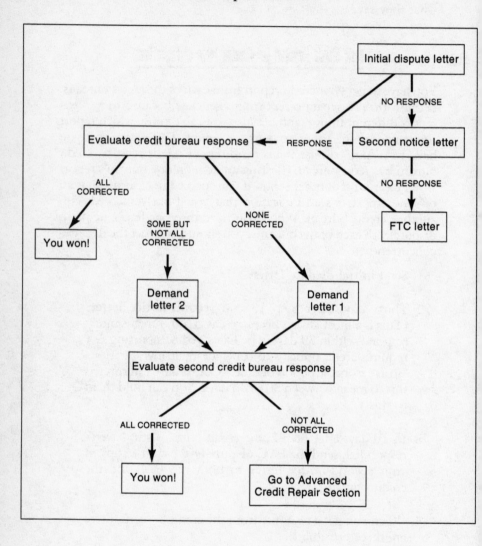

CHANGED AS ABOVE" (SPECIAL NOTE: Make sure that the changed item is now harmless; sometimes TRW will simply change it to a lesser derogatory. The harmless item should read "CURR ACC" [current account] or "PAID SAT" [paid satisfactorily] or "PAID ACC" [paid account]).

How to recognize this response from TransUnion or Equifax. This will appear on TransUnion and Equifax reports (they send you a new one at the end of the dispute) with the item removed or else the 30-60-90-day late pay indicators will all read 0. (See **Read Your Credit Report** for information on decoding the report.)

What to do next. Nothing, you've won.

b. They remove *some but not all* of the derogatory items that you disputed. This is a tactic for thwarting credit repair. *Don't settle for halfway.* Go to Step 5.

How to recognize this response from TRW. You'll know what's been corrected based on the criteria in 4a.

If TRW corrects the item on "CREDIT UPDATE," the account will now read "CURR ACC" (current account) or "PAID SAT" (paid satisfactorily) or "PAID ACC" (paid account). If the item has not been repaired, there will a comment "ITEM REMAINS, CONFIRMED BY SOURCE" or TRW will partially correct an item as some lesser degree of lateness. (See **Read Your Credit Report** for information on decoding the report.)

How to recognize this response from TransUnion or Equifax. Equifax or TransUnion answer with a new credit report that will show some items repaired and some not. The repaired items will either be removed or else the 30-60-90-day late pay indicators will all read 0. The unrepaired items will be repeated unchanged with no comment, be repeated with no 30-60-90 indicators and the comment "ITEM IN DISPUTE," or else the item will be repeated with less severe 30-60-90 indicators.

(See **Read Your Credit Report** for information on decoding the report.)

What to do next. Send **Demand Letter 2** to re-dispute the uncorrected items with stronger language that is rooted in your consumer rights. This works because your more specific complaints force the credit bureau to choose between an expensive investigation or clearing your credit. The credit bureaus have a limited number of roadblocks they're willing to enforce, and if you've gotten to this point you've already broken through one.

c. *None* of the items are corrected. Don't be frustrated. This is a common delaying tactic. Go to Step 6.

How to recognize this response from TRW. TRW will send you a "CREDIT UPDATE," on which it will say for each of the items you disputed, "item remains confirmed by source."

How to recognize this response from Trans-Union or Equifax. TransUnion or Equifax will send you a new copy of your credit report with the disputed items unchanged.

What to do next. Send **Demand Letter 1** to re-dispute the uncorrected items with stronger language that is rooted in your consumer rights. This works because your more specific complaints force the credit bureau to choose between an expensive investigation or clearing your credit. The credit bureaus have a limited number of roadblocks they're willing to enforce, and if you've gotten to this point you've already broken through one.

5. This step is only needed if you sent a **demand letter** (see 4b or 4c, above). Just as above—when you got a response from the credit bureau to your **initial dispute letter**—there are three possible responses from the credit bureau to your **demand letter**:

a. The remaining items have all been removed. You won!

b. Only some of them have been removed. Go to **Advanced Credit Repair**.

    c. None of them have been removed. Go to **Advanced Credit Repair**.

Basic Dispute Flowchart for Disputing Four or More Items

You have to get your credit report from each of the credit bureaus, because they're separate reporting agencies, because they often report different things, and because you can't know which report someone is going to use to deny you credit. This means that you have to dispute similar items on different credit reports, credit bureau by credit bureau. Clearing an item on one bureau's report won't clear it off another—but, if you succeed in clearing an item off one report, it's an indication that you'll likely succeed with another credit bureau.

    This flowchart is very similar to the flowchart for disputing three or fewer items. Because you never want to dispute more than three items at a time with any one credit bureau (it makes them suspicious), you can only begin with three at each bureau. This flowchart is different from the one for three or fewer items because it shows you how to add new items to the dispute process while you re-dispute old items.

    It's smart to dispute different items with different credit bureaus in order to determine which will most easily be removed from your credit history. For instance, if there are a total of nine bad items on your three credit reports, divide them up into three groups of three and dispute one group with each bureau. Re-dispute the ones that are removed first with the other bureaus. This across-the-board approach also helps determine which items need **advanced** strategies before wasting a lot of time playing out the **basic** written dispute process. (Even faster: Do the **advanced** disputes that you've identified while the other **basic** written disputes are still going on.) Across-the-board disputes will get you the cleanest credit, most quickly. This is important if you're in a hurry, i.e., to get a mortgage.

1. Send **initial dispute letter**. Remember, never dispute more than three items at a time! You'll have a chance to add more items later in this process, when initial disputes are resolved.

2. Thirty days after Step 1, send the **second-notice letter**. (This is almost always necessary, as credit bureaus rarely respond within 30 days. The Fair Credit Report Act requires credit bureaus to conclude their investigations "in a reasonable period of time." Courts have interpreted this to mean between 30 to 45 days. You can hold them to this.)

3. If, 10 days after Step 2, the credit bureaus still haven't responded, send the **FTC dispute letter** with a copy of your **second-notice letter** to both the FTC and the credit bureaus.

4. When you get a response from the credit bureaus, there are three possibilities:
   a. They remove *all* the initial derogatory items that you disputed. *You won this round!*

   How to recognize this response from TRW. This will appear on a TRW "credit update" as "ABOVE ITEM DELETED" or "ITEM CHANGED AS ABOVE" (SPECIAL NOTE: Make sure that the changed item is now harmless; sometimes TRW will simply change it to a lesser derogatory) with the harmless item now reading "CURR ACC" [current account] or "PAID SAT" [paid satisfactorily] or "PAID ACC" [paid account].

   How to recognize this response from TransUnion or Equifax. This will appear on TransUnion and Equifax reports (they send you a new one at the end of the dispute) with the item removed or else the 30-60-90-day late pay indicators will all read 0. (See **Read Your Credit Report** for information on decoding the report.)

   What to do next. Send your new disputes, starting again with the **initial dispute letter** (Step 1, above).
   b. They remove *some but not all* of the derogatory items that you disputed. This is a tactic for thwarting credit repair. *Don't settle for halfway.*

How to recognize this response from TRW.
You'll know what's been corrected based on the criteria in 4a. If TRW corrects the item on "CREDIT
UPDATE," the account will now read "CURR ACC"
[current account] or "PAID SAT" [paid satisfacto-
rily] or "PAID ACC" [paid account]. If the item
has not been repaired, there will a comment "ITEM
REMAINS CONFIRMED BY SOURCE" or TRW
will partially correct an item as some lesser degree of
lateness. (See **Read Your Credit Report** for information on decoding the report.)

**How to recognize this response from Equifax
or TransUnion.** You'll know what's been corrected
based on the criteria in 4a. Equifax or TransUnion
answer with a new credit report that will show some
items repaired and some not. The repaired items will
either be removed or else the 30-60-90-day late pay
indicators will all read 0. The unrepaired items will
be repeated unchanged with no comment, be repeated with no 30-60-90 indicators and the comment
"ITEM IN DISPUTE," or else the item will be repeated with less severe 30-60-90 indicators.

(See **Read Your Credit Report** for information
on decoding the report.)

What to do next. If you're following the across-
the-board strategy of disputing different items with
different credit bureaus, then play to your success—
dispute an item that was removed by one bureau with
the others. Hold the items that didn't come off to the
side for re-disputing later. Following this strategy,
you'll go back to the **initial dispute letter** (Step 1)
using all new items.

If, however, you have more items to dispute but
they are so few (one or two) that you want to re-
dispute the original rejected items immediately, send
the **secondary dispute letter**, in which you will add
the one or two new disputes to the original items that
weren't removed by your initial dispute.

The third possibility is that you've already successfully disputed at least three items and you don't have any more items to add, just items to re-dispute. Send **Demand Letter 2**.

c. *None* of the items are corrected. Don't be frustrated. This is a common delaying tactic.

How to recognize this response from TRW. TRW will send you a "CREDIT UPDATE," on which it will say for each of the items you disputed, "item remains confirmed by source."

How to recognize this response from Trans-Union or Equifax. TransUnion or Equifax will send you a new copy of your credit report with the disputed items unchanged.

What to do next. If you're following the across-the-board strategy of disputing different items with different credit bureaus, then play to your success—dispute an item that was removed by one bureau with the others. Hold the items that didn't come off to the side for re-disputing later. Following this strategy, you'll go back to the **initial dispute letter** (Step 1) using all new items.

The second possibility is that you have more items to dispute but they are so few (one or two) that you want to re-dispute one or two of the original rejected items immediately. In this case, send the **secondary dispute letter**, in which you will add the one or two new disputes to the original items that weren't removed by your initial dispute.

If however, you have no new items to dispute, send **Demand Letter 1** to re-dispute the uncorrected items with stronger language that is rooted in the your consumer rights. This works because your more specific complaints force the credit bureau to choose between an expensive investigation or clearing your credit. The credit bureaus have a limited number of roadblocks they're willing to enforce, and if you've gotten to this point you've already broken through one.

5. When you get a response to a **demand letter** or a **second-**

ary dispute letter (see Step 4, above), go back to Step 4 and evaluate your situation. Any item that you do not successfully dispute or re-dispute should be handled with techniques in the **Advanced Credit Repair** section.

Standard Credit Bureau Stalling Techniques

The law requires that credit bureaus respond to all written disputes. The credit bureaus stall for weeks and months using the following tricks:

1. They send you a form letter asking you to prove who you are by providing a copy of a utility or phone bill, in addition to Social Security number and current address. Solution: Include this information from the start so you can ignore the delaying tactic and proceed with the next step in the dispute process.
2. They send you a form letter telling you that they are investigating your complaint even when they are not. Solution: Ignore it and proceed with the next step in the dispute process.
3. They send you a form letter telling you that your complaint was not specific enough to investigate or correct. Solution: If you carefully follow the step-by-step instructions, your disputes will be clear and legally sound—so you can ignore the delaying tactic and proceed with the next step in the dispute process.
4. They just don't answer. Solution: Send your letters through certified mail from the start. If you haven't got an answer within six weeks, start over, but this time also send a copy of the dispute to the FTC using the FTC letter (see **FTC Dispute Letter**).

Basic Credit Bureau Disputes: Initial Dispute Letter

Instructions:

1. Put your name and address, with your Social Security number, anywhere on the page.

2. Put the credit bureau address on the same page. (Credit bureau addresses are listed in Appendix I, page 117.)

3. Include a photocopy of a recent bill (phone, electric, etc.) to prove that you are who you are at your address.

4. Write an opening paragraph to convey the following three points:
   a. There are errors.
   b. The errors are hurting your credit.
   c. The errors will potentially cause you to suffer some specific loss. Each case is different, and so you should, in one or two sentences, say what you personally stand to lose (i.e., a mortgage, an opportunity to buy something, a job because you can't get a car loan).

   Reminders: Dispute no more than three items at a time, and do not treat this as a form letter to be copied word-for-word. If you do, the credit bureaus may recognize that you are using a credit repair strategy and give you a hard time.

5. Give the name of the creditor that reported bad credit on you, and your account number with that creditor. List each creditor, account number, and dispute separately if you are disputing more than one item.

6. The specific reason why the credit item is wrong. You should remember that the reason itself will likely never be evaluated since it's usually too much trouble to sort out your differences with a creditor. Maybe:
   • It's not yours. Have you been confused with someone else? The credit bureaus usually can correct this problem very quickly since it's so easy for them to check. See **If You Suspect That the Credit Bureau Is Confusing You with Someone Else.**
   • There was a billing problem. You were billed at the wrong address, you questioned a bill (you never ordered the merchandise, it wasn't the right item . . .), or a payment wasn't properly credited to your account.

The credit bureaus have difficulty evaluating these challenges, and often take your word for it if you are persistent.

- You're certain that you always paid your account on time, and you can prove it with canceled checks or some other documentation. The credit bureaus don't ignore proof for very long.

The credit bureaus rarely correct a harmful item if you accept the blame for the problem ("I was out of work," "I was sick").

7. Close the letter by signing your name.

8. Send the letter through *certified/return receipt* mail. Otherwise the credit bureau will know that you don't have legal proof of having sent the letter, and may ignore it.

Initial Dispute Sample Letter

The specific reason given for why the above item (the Lone Star Bank Corp.) was in error is in this case a blanket denial. See Step 6 in the **Initial Dispute Letter Instructions** for more information.

your name
your address
your phone #
your Soc. Sec. #

date

Customer Service
credit bureau name
credit bureau address

Dear Customer Service:

The following errors are hurting my chances of ever getting a home for my family. If you don't correct them soon, I will lose a $30,000 deposit.

This account is wrong:

LONE STAR BANK CORP. account number 4483847293472394.

The Lone Star bank account is not a bad account. Your report says that I was late 60 days twice. I always pay this account on time.

I expect your prompt answer in writing.

Yours,
Joy Q. Public

Basic Credit Bureau Disputes: Second-Notice Letter

Use this letter to follow up your **initial dispute letter** if you get no response after a month.

Instructions:

1. Send a copy of the **initial dispute letter**, either reprinted, rewritten, or photocopied. Include a photocopy of the green postal receipt from your certified letter, or at least note the date you sent the **initial dispute letter.**
2. In your own words, add a notice to the copy that this is the second time you are sending it.
3. Send this letter one month after sending the **initial dispute letter.**
4. Send the letter through *certified/return receipt* mail. Otherwise the credit bureau will know that you don't have legal proof of having sent the letter, and may ignore it.

your name
your address
your phone #
your Soc. Sec. #

date

Customer Service
credit bureau name
credit bureau address

Dear Customer Service:

What's going on? It's been a month since I sent you the letter below! (A photocopy of my certified mail receipt is attached.) By law you must respond within a certain amount of time. I'm counting the days.

The following errors are hurting my chances of ever getting a home for my family. If you don't correct them soon, I will lose a $30,000 deposit.

This account is wrong:

LONE STAR BANK CORP. account number 4483847293472394.

The Lone Star bank account is not a bad account. Your report says that I was late 60 days twice. I always pay this account on time.

I expect your prompt answer in writing.

Yours,
Joy Q. Public

Basic Credit Bureau Disputes: Demand Letter 1

This letter is to be used if the credit bureau responds to either your **initial dispute letter** or **second-notice letter** with a refusal to correct *any of the items* on your report. If the credit bureau corrects some but not others, use **Demand Letter 2**. If the credit bureau corrected some or all of the items, and you want to dispute more items, use **secondary dispute letter**.

Instructions:

1. Put your name and address, with your Social Security number, anywhere on the page.

2. Put the credit bureau address on the same page. (Credit bureau addresses are listed in Appendix I, page 117.)

3. Write an opening paragraph to convey the following three points:
   a. "You have ignored my complaints of errors in my credit report."
   b. "The errors have hurt me financially and are continuing to do so."
   c. State the ways in which you have been financially penalized for their error. Each case is different, and so you should, in one or two sentences, say what you personally stand to lose (i.e., a mortgage, an opportunity to buy something, a job because you can't get a car loan).

   Reminders: Dispute no more than three items at a time, and do not treat this as a form letter to be copied word-for-word. If you do, the credit bureaus may recognize that you are using a credit repair strategy and give you a hard time.

4. Give the name of the creditor that reported bad credit on you, and your account number with that creditor. List each creditor, account number, and dispute separately if you are disputing more than one item.

your name
your address
your phone #
your Soc. Sec. #

date

Customer Service
credit bureau name
credit bureau address

Dear Customer Service:

I recently wrote you to have an item investigated on my credit report. You claim that you have verified that the item is correct as stated on the report. I don't how that could be true, since the item is wrong. You seem to have merely repeated the information.

Either correct the problem, or I will take whatever actions are needed to defend myself. This may include holding you responsible for my financial losses.

This account is wrong:

LONE STAR BANK CORP. account number 4483847293472394.

The Lone Star bank account is not a bad account. Your report says that I was late 60 days twice. I paid this account on time. Please tell me how I can contact the person who is supplying you with this information.

As I understand the law, you are liable for this error. If you don't correct the mistake immediately I will take stronger action.

Yours,
Joy Q. Public

5. State the specific reason why the credit item is wrong. Use the explanation and logic from the **initial dispute letter.** You may want to go into more detail this time.

6. Explain in your own words that you are going to take stronger action if you don't get satisfaction (i.e., call your lawyer, sue in small claims court, report the credit bureau to the Federal Trade Commission or your attorney general).

7. Close the letter by signing your name.

8. Send the letter through *certified/return receipt* mail. Otherwise the credit bureau will know that you don't have legal proof of having sent the letter, and may ignore it.

Basic Credit Bureau Disputes: Demand Letter 2

This letter is to be used if the credit bureau responds to either your **initial dispute letter** or **second-notice letter** with a refusal to correct *some of the items* on your report. If the credit bureau refuses to correct any of the items, use **Demand Letter 1**. If the credit bureau corrects all or only some of the items, and you want to dispute more items, use **secondary dispute**.

Instructions:

1. Put your name and address, with your social security number, anywhere on the page.

2. Put the credit bureau address on the same page. (Credit bureau addresses are listed in Appendix I, page 117.)

3. Write an opening paragraph to convey the following three points:
   a. "You have ignored my complaints of errors in my credit report."
   b. "The errors have hurt me financially and are continuing to do so."
   c. State the ways in which you have been financially penalized for their error. Each case is different, and so you should, in one or two sentences, say what you personally stand to lose (i.e., a mortgage, an opportunity to buy something, a job because you can't get a car loan).

   Reminders: Dispute no more than three items at a time, and do not treat this as a form letter to be copied word-for-word. If you do, the credit bureaus may recognize that you are using a credit repair strategy and give you a hard time.

4. Give the name of the creditor that reported bad credit on you, and your account number with that creditor. List each creditor, account number, and dispute separately if you are disputing more than one item.

5. State the specific reason why the credit item is wrong. Use the explanation and logic from the **initial dispute letter**. You may want to go into more detail this time.

6. Explain in your own words that you are going to take stronger action if you don't get satisfaction (i.e., call your lawyer, sue in small claims court, report the credit bureau to the Federal Trade Commission or your attorney general).

7. Close the letter by signing your name.

8. Send the letter through *certified/return receipt* mail. Otherwise the credit bureau will know that you don't have legal proof of having sent the letter, and may ignore it.

your name
your address
your phone #
your Soc. Sec. #

date

Customer Service
credit bureau name
credit bureau address

Dear Customer Service:

In the most recent update of my report, I see that you have corrected some of your mistakes, but not all. This isn't a case of some right and some wrong. They were all wrong.

You claim that you have verified the items, but I don't how that could be true, since they are still in error. You seem to have merely repeated the information.

This account is still wrong:

LONE STAR BANK CORP. account number 4483847293472394.

The Lone Star bank account is not a bad account. Your report says that I was late 60 days twice. I paid this account on time. Please tell me how I can contact the person who is supplying you with this information.

As I understand the law, you are liable for this error. If you don't correct the mistake immediately I will take stronger action.

Yours,
Joy Q. Public

Basic Credit Bureau Disputes: Secondary Dispute Letter

This letter is to be used if the credit bureau responds to either your **initial dispute letter** or **second-notice letter** by correcting some or all of the items, *and you want to dispute more items*. This letter is especially useful if you have many items to dispute and do not want to arouse the suspicions of the credit bureaus by disputing many items all at once.

If the credit bureau refuses to correct any of the items, use **Demand Letter 1**. If the credit bureau corrects some items, but leaves others, use **Demand Letter 2**.

Instructions:

1. Put your name and address, with your Social Security number, anywhere on the page.

2. Put the credit bureau address on the same page. (Credit bureau addresses are listed in Appendix I, page 117.)

3. Include a photocopy of a recent bill (phone, electric, etc.) to prove that you are who you are at your address.

4. Write an opening paragraph to convey the following three points:
   a. "Thanks for correcting items, but I've found some more errors in my research."
   b. "The remaining errors are hurting my credit."
   c. State that the errors will potentially cause you to suffer some specific loss. Each case is different, and so you should, in one or two sentences, say what you personally stand to lose (i.e., a mortgage, an opportunity to buy something, a job because you can't get a car loan).

Reminders: Dispute no more than three items at a time, and do not treat this as a form letter to be copied word-for-word. If you do, the credit bureaus may recognize that you are using a credit repair strategy and give you a hard time.

your name
your address
your phone #
your Soc. Sec. #

date

Customer Service
credit bureau name
credit bureau address

Dear Customer Service:

Your reports are so confusing that I've only now identified another error on my credit report.

The item in error is:

FIRST AMERICA CREDIT CARD account number 47252361293.

Your report says that I was 30 days late once, but that's not my fault. That payment was late because I did not receive a bill. The bill was sent to a former address even though I had notified the company in writing that I moved.

I look forward to a prompt remedy of this unpleasantness.

Yours,
Joy Q. Public

5. Give the name of the creditor that reported bad credit on you, and your account number with that creditor. List each creditor, account number, and dispute separately if you are disputing more than one item.

6. The specific reason why the credit item is wrong. Use the explanation and logic from the **initial dispute letter**. You may want to go into more detail this time.

7. Close the letter by signing your name.

8. Send the letter through *certified/return receipt* mail. Otherwise the credit bureau will know that you don't have legal proof of having sent the letter, and may ignore it.

FTC Dispute Letter

This letter is useful if the credit bureaus just don't seem to answer your written disputes within six weeks (the 45-day "reasonable time period" that the law gives the credit bureau to respond).

You are sending this letter so that you can also send a copy to each of the delaying credit bureaus to show that you mean business. Therefore, keep a few copies of this letter for that purpose.

(For more information about credit bureau stalling tactics and credit repair countermeasures, see **Standard Credit Bureau Stalling Techniques**.)

> *your name*
> *your address*
> *your phone #*
> *Social Security #*

Federal Trade Commission
Pennsylvania Ave. and 6th St. N.W.
Washington, DC 20580
(202) 326-2000

date

Dear Consumer Complaints:

Credit bureau name won't respond to my complaints about errors in my credit report. Enclosed is a copy of the written dispute, and a photocopy of the postal return receipt card. Please help in any way possible.

Yours truly,
J.Q. Public

You can also send a copy of this to your state attorney general's office, or your state department of consumer affairs.

Remember when using this letter, and all letters in this book, to:

1. Reword the letter in your own words. You don't want to appear like you are being coached or following a repair strategy.
2. Keep a photocopy of the letter for your records. The copies are often used later in the repair process.
3. Send the letter through *certified/return receipt mail*. This is proof that you sent the letter.

Basic Repair: If You Suspect That the Credit Bureau Is Confusing You with Someone Else

This is the most common and easiest problem to clear up. Send an **initial dispute letter** in which you clearly identify all items that are not yours. This is a special case in which you can dispute more than three items.

ADVANCED CREDIT REPAIR: INTRODUCTION

By this point in the steps to repairing your credit rating, you have received and decoded your credit reports from the three major credit bureaus. You have identified the harmful information they are reporting on you, and you are ready to change it.

You may have exhausted the **basic** dispute process, which is essentially a written correspondence with the credit bureaus. Or you may be in a rush, and you want to employ other techniques while the written disputes are running their course. If you're up to it, concurrent **basic** and **advanced** disputes are a good way of expediting the repair process.

The crux of the **advanced** techniques, which begin on the next page, is to understand the creditor who is reporting bad credit on you, and to develop strategies for your particular mix of bad credit items:

• items best disputed through the **basic** credit bureau techniques

- items best negotiated directly with the creditors
- knowing when to switch between credit bureau and creditor negotiations if one method is not working

Begin planning your repair strategy by assessing the types of creditors you're up against, and which are best suited to direct **advanced** disputes and which are best handled indirectly through **basic** disputes with the credit bureaus.

Choosing Basic or Advanced Techniques for Disputing a Derogatory Item

The following chart will help you decide whether to dispute a harmful piece of credit through the credit bureaus or with a creditor. In all cases, either way is better than no way, but if you take the time to locate your particular situation on the chart, you can plan the fastest, most effective dispute. Essentially you want to isolate items that can be negotiated with creditors because:

- a creditor's agreement to clear an item will clear the item with all three credit bureaus;
- the more disputed items you can resolve with the creditors, the easier time you will have with the credit bureaus, who become more resistant when you dispute many separate items simultaneously.

Creditors, and the type of credit they give, are the most important factors in planning a strong dispute. There are nine main kinds of creditors and credit, each with its own personality and vulnerabilities, running down the left side of the chart.

Other important factors in choosing a credit bureau or creditor dispute are:

- the age of the item. The credit bureaus often can't confirm older items even when they're true (because the creditors don't keep good archival records).
- the grouped or scattered nature of the latenesses in the 24-month history. Grouped latenesses are often attributed to one uncredited payment or billing error that caused subsequent payments to appear as late.

Legend

Age of Credit Items in Status Date or Date Verified:

- "O" Old (more than two years)
- "N" New (less than two years)

Lateness Patterns in the 24-Month History:

- "S" Scattered latenesses (not adjacent in time)
- "P" Patterned latenesses (grouped month after month)

Characterizations of Repair Prospects, from good to not:

- Excellent
- Good
- Possible
- Poor
- Impossible

	Credit Bureau Dispute	Creditor Negotiation	Comments
Retail Store Credit Department Store	O,S: Good. O,P: Excellent. N,S: Possible. N,P: Good.	O,S: Possible. O,P: Excellent. N,S: Possible. N,P: Excellent.	Customer-service orientation favors negotiation. Credit bureaus for older accounts.
Banks	O,S: Good. O,P: Excellent. N,S: Poor. N,P: Good.	O,S: Fair. O,P: Good. N,S: Poor. N,P: Possible.	Better to work through credit bureaus. Patterns are important.
MasterCard/Visa and Other Credit Cards	O,S: Good. O,P: Excellent. N,S: Possible. N,P: Good.	O,S: Possible. O,P: Good. N,S: Poor. N,P: Possible.	Patterns are important; problems in correct billing address and amounts lead to most corrections.
Mortgage Credit	O,S: Good. O,P: Excellent. N,S: Poor. N,P: Good.	O,S: Possible. O,P: Good. N,S: Poor. N,P: Possible.	Tough to fix. Older paid accounts most likely to repair. Negotiations o.k. if you persevere.

	Credit Bureau Dispute	Creditor Negotiation	Comments
Auto Loans	O,S: Possible. O,P: Good. N,S: Poor. N,P: Possible.	O,S: Poor. O,P: Possible. N,S: Poor. N,P: Poor.	Toughest to fix. Older paid accounts most likely to repair. Negotiations can work if you persevere.
Student Loan Agencies/ Universities	O,S: Good. O,P: Excellent. N,S: Possible. N,P: Good.	O,S: Possible. O,P: Possible. N,S: Possible. N,P: Possible.	Credit bureau disputes best. Bureaucracy discourages negotiation.
Medical (Dentists/ Doctors/Hospitals)	O,S: Good if paid. O,P: Good if paid. N,S: Good if paid. N,P: Good if paid.	O,S: Good if owe. O,P: Excellent if owe. N,S: Good if owe. N,P: Excellent if owe.	Negotiations best if you still owe money. Credit bureaus otherwise.
Collection Agencies	O,S: Good if paid. O,P: Excellent if paid. N,S: Possible if paid. N,P: Possible if paid.	O,S: Excellent if owe. O,P: Excellent if owe. N,S: Good if owe. N,P: Good if owe.	Negotiations best if you still owe money. Credit bureaus otherwise.
Public Records	O,S: Good. O,P: Good. N,S: Possible. N,P: Possible.	O,S: Impossible. O,P: Impossible. N,S: Impossible. N,P: Impossible.	Negotiations impossible; must work through credit bureaus.

Creditor Type: Retail Stores

NOTE: If a retail debt is with a collection agency, also refer to the **Collection Agency** section.

RETAIL STORE BACKGROUND

The largest department stores are the source of many bad credit items. Retail credit is an important indicator of how you pay your bills and how you view credit. The stores are aggressive about reporting credit because they have essentially no leverage in getting you to pay, short of getting a court to force you.

The credit that retailers give you is called "unsecured credit" because they've given you goods such as clothes, electronics, or furniture, and they really only have your promise that you'll someday give them money.

By reporting any lateness in your payment history, and especially any failure to pay, retailers are usually successful in eventually getting money from deadbeats. As the retailer's reasoning goes, someday the deadbeat will want to buy a house or get a car loan. Then they'll have to pay the outstanding money.

The consistent reporting of latenesses also works to the retailer's advantage. If enough credit customers understand that the late paying will count against them, more people will pay on time. The fear of bad credit gets customers who do pay on time to continue doing so.

RETAIL STORE STRATEGY

With a handful of exceptions such as Sears and JCPenney, many retailers will clear your credit if you approach them through their customer service departments and negotiate. Customer service departments clear customer credit every day; it is part of their job.

Even if you still owe money, call up customer service and ask plainly to have your credit record restored to good health. Your leverage with the retailers is twofold: they want to be paid, and they want to keep you as a customer.

When you request to have your credit cleared, you may want to tell them that their negative report is preventing you from buying a car or house. Be insistent. Remind them that you have been a loyal customer, and that you don't want to have to take your business elsewhere because of a simple misunderstanding (always call it a misunderstanding). Work your way up to a supervisor if necessary, and while keeping your cool, let them hear a hint of the irate customer who could be made happy, that is, if this little credit problem gets straightened out right away.

Retail stores succumb to the wear-'em-down technique more than most creditors. Stick to it even when all seems hopeless, because, as in all credit situations, the system is not set up for people who won't take no for an answer.

You may want to consult **Notes on Retail Store Negotiations** (page 76) in further developing your strategy.

1. Initial Negotiation.
   a. If you're up-to-date in your payments: make this part of your case with customer service. Some stores will just roll over and say, "Well, you're paid in full, we'll be happy to clear the credit."

      Others will say, depending on how bad the credit was, that they won't clear it up—that it's history, and you can't change history. This is more likely if you were very delinquent or if the matter proceeded to a lawsuit or judgment against you. If the creditor won't budge, skip to Step 2 below.
   b. If you owe money that you are willing to repay: ask the retailer to clear your credit upon repayment. Include the **"restrictively endorsed" settlement letter** with your check, and modify the letter to the specific terms you've negotiated with the retailer.
   c. If you owe more money than you are willing or able to repay immediately: negotiate using the logic of the **"debt schedule" settlement letter**. You are offering to repay the money according to a strict schedule; you are asking to have your credit cleared, the repayment terms extended, and, possibly, to have the debt reduced.

2. If negotiations don't go well with the customer service departments: you can dictate your own terms to them using the **"restrictively endorsed" settlement letter**,

provided that they cash the check you enclose. You can also use the **"debt schedule"** settlement letter.

3. Follow up the settlement letter with a letter to the credit bureaus (see **Advanced Credit Bureau Dispute: Documentation Letter**) to make sure that they ultimately remove the derogatory items you have negotiated off with the creditors.

Notes on Retail Store Negotiations

The following negotiating strategies are tailored to retail reporting disputes involving specific problems with retail store debt (like credit cards, also known as revolving debt).

Retail stores have layers of customer service. You will most likely reach the person who can help you through an 800 number at a remote site. Unlike almost all other creditors, retail stores will sometimes clear your credit as a simple matter of courtesy. Ask for it first. If customer service says no, it's time to negotiate.

Direct negotiations with retailers work best when:

- You owe money. Offer to pay in exchange for clearing your credit.
- You have irrefutable proof of a creditor error. It could be anything—the couch never came, you didn't order it, etc. The retailer should obviously correct their mistake. You'll still want to follow up with the credit bureaus since the retailer already proved that it was sloppy.
- There is only one lateness showing. It might not be your fault. The system of crediting and slow mail shouldn't work against you. Everybody deserves a second chance. Don't forget to follow up with the credit bureaus yourself.
- You changed your billing address. You can't be late for not paying what you don't know about, even if retailer argues otherwise. See **Revolving Credit—Change of Billing Address Letter**.
- You asked for a bill to be clarified. You can't be late for

not paying what you questioned (although you must continue to pay uncontested bills). See **Revolving Credit—Billing Clarification Letter.**

Just as you should follow up all successful negotiations with letters to the credit bureaus, you should also follow up unsuccessful negotiations with letters to the credit bureaus. Sometimes clearly stating your side of the story is enough to prompt a credit bureau to remove an item that the creditor still insists on. If the credit bureau doesn't want to pick sides, it will simply drop the item from your report. See **Advanced Credit Bureau Dispute: Documentation Letter**.

Creditor Type: Banks and Mortgage Lenders

BANK BACKGROUND

Because their business is loaning money, banks aggressively report credit items. The credit reporting industry was created in large part to aid banks in making lending decisions.

Although banks often grant "secured credit"—meaning that they can attach specific items such as your house or car to a loan agreement—they are still vulnerable to your failure to keep a payment promise.

Credit reporting is an important tool that banks use to insure they get paid. Banking is also a highly regulated industry. For these reasons, it is difficult to negotiate with a bank. It's much harder for a bank to cut an individual a break because they are required to treat customers equally.

BANK STRATEGY

Bank negotiations are difficult. Except in cases where you have absolute proof that the bank is in error, you are better off disputing a bad bank credit item with a credit bureau. Nevertheless, there is some wiggle room for negotiation.

If you can, build a relationship with an individual who can help you. Polite pestering can get you far with banks, at least to the point where it's easier for them to clear your credit than answer your calls.

Banks sometimes agree to remove bad credit in exchange for payment of past due money, especially if you can demonstrate, to some degree, that there was a problem in the billing. Maybe they weren't notifying you at your correct address or at least the one you asked them to change billing to. Sticking to your story, and couching it in the terms covered later in this book (see **Using the Fair Billing Act**) will go a long way toward getting a bank, or any credit department for that matter, to see your side and fix the offending credit item.

You may want to consult **Notes on Bank and Mortgage Lender Negotiations** (page 79) in further developing your strategy.

1. Initial Negotiation.
   a. If you're fully paid up on the loan, with no remaining payments: forget about disputing with the bank; do a **basic** credit bureau dispute. You will want to include a copy of the **"restrictively endorsed" settlement letter** if you included one with your final payment (see **Advanced Credit Bureau Dispute: Documentation Letter**).
   b. If you owe money that you are willing to repay: ask the bank to clear your credit upon repayment. If they really want the money, they'll cut this deal. Include a **"restrictively endorsed" settlement letter** with your check, and modify the letter to the specific terms you've negotiated with the bank.

   Even if the bank won't agree to clear your credit upon repayment, you can try dictating the terms by enclosing a **"restrictively endorsed" settlement letter** with a payment. Many larger institutions automatically process incoming checks, and thereby agree to your terms by default. Mortgage lenders, and many banks too, tend to return restrictively endorsed checks. If your check is returned, make your payment without restrictive endorsement right away to avoid further latenesses, and pursue your dispute with the credit bureaus. The settlement letter can still be useful (see **Advanced Credit Bureau Dispute: Documentation Letter**).

    c. If you owe more money than you are willing or able to repay immediately: negotiate using the logic of the **"debt schedule" settlement letter**. You are offering to repay the money according to a strict schedule; you are asking to have your credit cleared, the repayment terms extended, and, possibly, to have the debt reduced. Many banks routinely accept seventy-cents-on-the-dollar settlements, but settlements as low as thirty cents on the dollar are possible.

2. Follow up the settlement letter with a letter to the credit bureaus (see **Advanced Credit Bureau Dispute: Documentation Letter**) to make sure that they ultimately remove the derogatory items you have negotiated off with the creditors.

Notes on Bank and Mortgage Lender Negotiations

The following negotiating strategies are tailored to credit reporting disputes involving specific problems with installment debt. These debts typically involve a coupon book or payment agreement that says you will forego your right of bill notification before each payment.

    Banks, like retail stores, have layers of customer service. You will most likely reach the person who can help you through an 800 number at a remote site. They are different than retailers, though, because they won't generally agree to remove a derogatory credit item just because it's paid or older. For this reason, we don't recommend negotiating by phone with banks.

    Direct bank negotiations work best when:

- You have irrefutable proof of a bank error. They should obviously correct their mistake. You'll still want to follow up with the credit bureaus since the bank already admitted that it was sloppy.
- There is only one lateness showing. It might not be your fault. The system of crediting and slow mail shouldn't work against you. Everybody deserves a second chance. Don't forget to follow up with the credit bureaus yourself.

- There are a number of latenesses but they are all in a row, month-after-month. You can argue that this is caused by only one uncredited payment, which would cause every payment thereafter to be listed as "30 days late." Because this problem involves a payment lost in the system, you don't have a canceled check or other proof. This shouldn't stop you from pressing your case. Again, don't forget to follow up with the credit bureaus yourself.

Just as you should follow up all successful negotiations with letters to the credit bureaus, you should also follow up unsuccessful negotiations with letters to the credit bureaus. Sometimes clearly stating your side of the story is enough to prompt a credit bureau to remove an item that the creditor still insists on. If the credit bureau doesn't want to pick sides, it will simply drop the item from your report. See **Advanced Credit Bureau Dispute: Documentation Letter**.

Creditor Type: Credit Cards
(MasterCard/Visa/Discover/American Express)

CREDIT CARD BACKGROUND

Credit card companies are vulnerable because the credit they issue is unsecured with other property, money, or merchandise. As such they are consistent reporters of any lateness or failure to pay.

Bad credit from credit cards mars many credit reports. Credit reporting is an important tool that card companies use to insure that they get paid. The industry is also highly regulated, and therefore difficult to negotiate with. It's much harder for a credit card lender to cut an individual a break because it is required to treat customers equally.

The good news is that credit card companies are overburdened and increasingly unprofitable. They are often hungry to settle outstanding debts; sometimes for less than the total amount, frequently for the removal of bad credit.

CREDIT CARD STRATEGY

Credit card negotiations are difficult, but the requirement that you be billed accurately and at the address that you state creates some wiggle room. If a bill isn't sent to a correct billing address, or if a consumer seeks to clarify billing amounts, payment cannot be reported as late.

You can learn about the tools at your disposal (see **Fair Billing Act, Revolving Credit—Change of Billing Address Letter**, and **Revolving Credit—Billing Clarification Letter**) now, or follow the negotiation how-to and use them as they are needed.

If you can, build a relationship with an individual who can help you. Polite pestering can get you far with credit card companies, at least to the point where it's easier for them to clear your credit than answer your calls.

Credit-card companies sometimes agree to remove bad credit in exchange for payment of past due money, especially if you can demonstrate, to some degree, that there was a problem in the billing. See **Notes on Credit Card Negotiations**.

1. Initial Negotiation.
   a. If you're fully paid up on a card account that has been closed but had latenesses: forget about disputing latenesses with the credit card company; do a **basic** credit bureau dispute. You will want to include a copy of the **"restrictively endorsed" settlement letter** if you included one with your final payment (see **Advanced Credit Bureau Dispute: Documentation Letter**).
   b. If you are willing and able to repay money on a unsettled card account that has been closed (that had latenesses): The longer it's been, the more likely they are to clear your credit upon payment, especially if you argue about billing errors. (See **Notes on Credit Card Negotiations**.)
   c. If you are not willing or able to repay money on a unsettled card account (open or closed) that had latenesses: negotiate using the logic of the **"debt schedule" settlement letter**. You are offering to repay the money according to a strict schedule; you are asking to have your credit cleared, the repayment terms extended, and, possibly, to have the debt reduced. Many credit card companies routinely accept seventy-cents-on-the-dollar settlements, but

settlements as low as thirty cents on the dollar are possible.

OPEN ACCOUNTS

d. If you're a current customer with late payments on your record but you are willing to repay the current due: send a **"restrictively endorsed" settlement letter** with your payment. You are dictating the terms by enclosing a **"restrictively endorsed" settlement letter** with a payment. Many larger institutions automatically process incoming checks, and thereby agree to your terms by default.

Credit card companies rarely return restrictively endorsed checks. If your check is returned, make your payment without restrictive endorsement right away to avoid further latenesses, and pursue your dispute with the credit bureaus. The settlement letter can still be useful (see **Advanced Credit Bureau Dispute: Documentation Letter**).

2. Follow up the settlement letter with a letter to the credit bureaus (see **Advanced Credit Bureau Dispute: Documentation Letter**) to make sure that they ultimately remove the derogatory items you have negotiated off with the creditors.

Notes on Credit Card Negotiations

The following negotiating strategies are tailored to credit reporting disputes involving specific problems with credit card debt (also known as revolving debt).

Credit card companies, like retail stores, have layers of customer service. You will most likely reach the person who can help you through an 800 number at a remote site. They are different from retailers, though, because they won't generally agree to remove a derogatory credit item just because it's paid or it's so old that records are no longer kept—unless you still owe them some money that they don't expect to collect.

Direct negotiations with credit card companies work best when:

- you have irrefutable proof of a credit card company error. They should obviously correct their mistake. You'll still want to follow up with the credit bureaus since the card company already admitted that it was sloppy.
- there is only one lateness showing. It might not be your fault. The system of crediting and slow mail shouldn't work against you. Everybody deserves a second chance. Don't forget to follow up with the credit bureaus yourself.
- you changed your billing address. You can't be late for not paying what you don't know about, even if credit card companies argue otherwise. See **Revolving Credit—Change of Billing Address Letter**.
- you asked for a bill to be clarified. You can't be late for not paying what you questioned (although you must continue to pay uncontested bills). See **Revolving Credit—Billing Clarification Letter**.

Just as you should follow up all successful bank negotiations with letters to the credit bureaus, you should also follow up unsuccessful negotiations with letters to the credit bureaus. Sometimes clearly stating your side of the story is enough to prompt a credit bureau to remove an item that the creditor still insists on. See **Advanced Credit Bureau Dispute: Documentation Letter**.

Creditor Type: Auto Loans

AUTO LOAN BACKGROUND

Car lending is unique in the credit world. Because cars are so expensive to stock in inventory and so easy to repossess, car loans are often made to people who might not, for instance, qualify for a mortgage. However, like mortgages, car loans are classified as installment debt. Under most car loan agreements, you are not billed each month for your payment; you are expected to send it in on your own.

Car loan criteria are flexible enough so that people with little or no credit can qualify. Often this involves a co-signer for the young buyer. Another common device is for the dealer to finance the car for you, instead of using a more rigid bank or major automotive lending institution.

Predictably, this easy sell gives way to heavy collection tactics that include aggressive credit reporting. Late and missed car payments mar many credit reports and are often the stumbling block to getting more credit.

AUTO LOAN STRATEGY

It's next to impossible to negotiate clean credit from an auto loan lender because the lender can always repossess the car if you owe money. (There are some extra considerations discussed in **Notes on Auto Loan Negotiations**.)

Except in cases where you have absolute proof that the lender is in error, you are better off disputing a bad auto loan credit item (such as "voluntary surrender," "repossession," or latenesses) with a credit bureau (see **Basic Credit Bureau Dispute**).

Because the loan is dead, credit bureaus will sometimes not be able to verify the item and be forced to clear it. That said, it's unlikely you'll ever get a "voluntary surrender" or "repossession" removed from your report. If the credit bureau is able to verify the item after repeated disputes as detailed in the **basic** section, exercise your right to have an explanation (no more than 100 words) appended to your credit report. See **Advanced Credit Repair: Sample Explanation Letter**.

If you have a documented reason why the late marks are wrong that amounts to absolute proof the lender made an error in crediting your account, or if you were late by a day or so just once or twice, you might prevail in a phone negotiation to get the credit straightened out.

NOTES ON AUTO LOAN NEGOTIATIONS

Even though it's next to impossible to negotiate with auto loan lenders, it can still be helpful to know how inflexible they are.

If you miss a payment, you are guilty until proven innocent. Payments sent during the grace period are sometimes recorded as late. Other errors do occur, such as an uncredited payment. You should fight these.

Take care with these people, though. It is especially important to maintain your payments while waiting for an insurance settlement for any car theft or damage issue, even if that settlement is guaranteed. Your agreements with insurance companies are independent of your responsibility to make loan payments. Unlike many other lenders, auto lenders usually refuse to delete bad credit, even if you have documentation (for instance, police and accident reports or repair bills) that the car doesn't work or was stolen.

When plotting credit repair efforts and dealing with auto lenders, expect them to be inflexible. Your best bet is the credit bureaus.

Creditor Type: Student Loan Agencies

NOTE: If a student loan is with a collection agency, consider skipping to the **Collection Agency** section.

STUDENT LOAN BACKGROUND

Education loans are often guaranteed by the government, although they originate at banks and student loan agencies (depending on what state you live in). Like most bank loans, they are installment loans, which means that you owe a payment whether or not you are billed for it. These are distinguished from most credit card loan agreements.

Most student loan agreements allow for forbearance—the right to begin repayment some time in the future (i.e., when you graduate). The rules on when you begin paying back these loans vary with your economic situation, your job status, the time since you've completed school, and any public services that you may have performed.

Typical student loan problems begin when borrowers don't keep lenders informed that they are still within the scope of the forbearance. You might still be in graduate school, but if you forget to tell the bank, they may list you as having defaulted on your undergraduate loan.

The complex mix of lenders and guarantors often leads to disastrous mistakes when loans are categorized as defaults. One incorrectly defaulted loan becomes many derogatory credit marks as the guarantor takes over and passes the debt to a collection attorney, who in turn gets a court judgment against you. Each step generates its own bad credit item.

STUDENT LOAN STRATEGY

The student loan system is notorious, even in the credit world, for being impossible to work with. Not only is it excruciatingly impersonal, but there are usually many parties involved. Unlike other creditors, even when you get one or more of the lenders/ guarantors to agree to correct your credit, they won't necessarily follow through.

The chaotic system can work in your favor because it makes it extremely difficult for the credit bureaus to confirm information that you dispute and demand to have investigated. Therefore, *the most consistently effective strategy is to work at the credit bureau level*. (There are some other considerations, though, discussed in **Notes on Student Loan Negotiations**.) At the same time, stay current with your payment agreement to head off new problems.

Finally, as we noted at the top of this section, if the student loan is in collection, you may want to skip to the **Collection Agency** section. You can also follow these creditor negotiation steps, but include a **"Creditor's agreement to clear collection account" letter** with any settlement.

1. Initial Negotiation.
   a. If the only problem with your student loan (ongoing or fully paid-back) is a few latenesses: you can try explaining away the bad marks with the lender (see **Notes on Bank and Mortgage Lender Negotiations**), but you should also conduct your dispute with the credit bureaus (see Item 2, below).
   b. If your student loan (ongoing or fully paid-back) ever went into default: if you have copies of forbearance letters that the lender claims not to have received, you can send them to the lender, but you should also conduct your dispute with the credit bureaus (see Item 2, below).

2. Credit Bureau Disputes. As explained in the strategy above, you should conduct student loan disputes at the credit bureau level (see **Basic**). This has the advantage of

often getting related bad marks off your reports without having to talk to each party in the student loan chain.

You may also want to see the **student loan "forbearance notification" letter** and **advanced credit bureau dispute: documentation letter** if you have any supporting materials.

NOTES ON STUDENT LOAN NEGOTIATIONS

Student loans have a nasty habit of ending up in court when they're not dealt with. If you have a judgment against you because of your student loan, see **Public Records**.

Before you are sued, student loans are put into "default" status. This usually means that the loan is taken over by a state or federal student loan agency's collection department. These bureaucratic organizations are lousy at fixing mistakes. Be skeptical about any promise that you do not get in writing, and do not be surprised if you never get a promise in writing. Treat them as an especially dangerous collection agency because they can get a judgment against you without notification under the terms on many student loan agreements (see **Public Records** for more about judgments).

Creditor Type: Medical (Dentist/Doctor/Lab/Hospital)

MEDICAL BACKGROUND

The credit reporting and collection systems associated with health care are just as messed up as the health-care system as a whole. For this reason, medical credit items are included in this book even though they do not, unlike the other creditors discussed, involve some kind of credit agreement. (The negotiation steps below are also useful for dealing with other small creditors who may have handed your account over to a collection agency.)

Slow medical payments do not ordinarily show up on credit reports until the doctor hands the account over to a collection agency or sues. This often happens automatically if the account goes 60 days past due. Thanks to the crazy health-care system, many consumers don't learn of medical bills from third-party providers like labs and specialists until they become collection accounts and damage the consumer's credit.

MEDICAL STRATEGY

When you have a bad debt arising from unpaid health care, you usually have both the collection agency and the doctor to deal with, and possibly a public record.

Most doctors will agree to clear your credit if you pay them the money that you owe (or at least begin repaying the money as part of a repayment schedule). But you will still have to deal with the collection agency if there's one involved. If you don't do anything, the collection agency will probably classify the debt as a "paid collection account," which is bad. It is, therefore, extremely important to discuss and include the **"creditor's agreement to clear collection account" letter** as part of any settlement.

1a. If you owe money that you are able to pay in a lump sum: ask the doctor to clear your credit upon repayment. Include the **"creditor's agreement to clear collection account" letter** with your check, and modify the letter to the specific terms you've negotiated with the doctor.

1b. If you owe more money than you are willing or able to repay immediately: follow the same logic of **1a** but include the logic of the **"debt schedule" settlement letter**. You are offering to repay the money according to a strict schedule; you are asking to have your credit cleared, the repayment terms extended, and, possibly, to have the debt reduced. Settlements of seventy cents on the dollar are common, but settlements as low as thirty cents on the dollar are possible. Offers of full payment will expedite the process.

2. If the collection account is already paid: you can ask the creditor to agree to a version of **"creditor's agreement to clear collection account" letter** (take out the part about enclosing a check).

If that doesn't work, dispute the item through the credit bureaus (see **Basic Dispute**). There are many reasons why an account could be put into collection improperly. Maybe you weren't billed at the right address, or maybe the creditor ignored your requests for clarification of a bill (see **Fair Credit Billing Act**).

3. Follow up the settlement letter with a letter to the credit bureaus (see **Advanced Credit Bureau Dispute: Documentation Letter**) to make sure that they ultimately remove the derogatory items you have negotiated off with the creditors.

Creditor Type: Debt Collection Agencies

BACKGROUND

The business of collection agencies is collecting money. They're good at it. The people who work in collections are a distinct subculture with their own lingo and posturing. They talk tough and they push every advantage they have. "Working the client" is the euphemism for a process of intimidation that skirts consumer laws. Phone calls, letters, veiled threats, and even talking to co-workers, family, and neighbors are all collection techniques.

Don't be intimidated by any of this. As with any other debt, you should negotiate the terms of repayment with your needs (and rights) in mind.

(For more background, see **Notes on Collection Agency Negotiations**, page 91.)

STRATEGY

1a. If you owe money that you are able to pay in a lump sum: try working with the original creditor using the appropriate creditor background section and the **"creditor's agreement to clear collection account" letter**.

   If that doesn't work, send in the payment to the collection agency as a restrictively endorsed check using a **"restrictively endorsed" settlement letter**.

   If the collection agency cashes the check, you've won. Skip to Step 3, below.

   If the collection agency balks at the restrictive endorsement and doesn't deposit the check, they will call. (You included your phone number in the settlement letter.)

   Many collection agencies take the position that a legitimate collection account cannot be deleted from your credit reports. They may also say that only the original creditor can decide to have the bad credit removed. These arguments are specious. As a matter of settlement, any item of bad credit can be deleted.

If the collection agency refuses to help clear your credit, there are several approaches that sometimes turn the agency around:

• You can call into question the validity of the original collection action. Maybe you weren't billed at the right address (see **Fair Credit Billing Act**) or maybe you think you already paid the debt, but it's so long ago that you don't have the canceled check. Add "Just to settle the matter, I will pay but you can't ruin my credit because of this error." Push the argument to a supervisor.

• Demand that the debt be returned to the original creditor for you to work out repayment terms. Use the **cease communication letter**.

In the end, they want to be paid and it doesn't cost them anything to agree to clear your credit. The above explanations give them an excuse to accommodate you.

• If they still won't agree, hire an attorney (see **Appendix VII: Using a Lawyer**). A skilled lawyer can often enforce your rights better than you can. Again, collection agencies want to collect money, not fight lawyers. Remember: Although you are willing to pay, you must get your credit cleared in the process. That's your goal.

• If they do agree to your settlement terms, make sure you get the agreement in writing or use your same **"restrictively endorsed" settlement letter** again. Collection agencies tend not to follow up on their promises to clear your credit, so you will want to send this documentation to the credit bureaus once you have it. Go to Step 3, below.

1b. If you owe more money than you are willing or able to repay immediately: first try working a deal with the original creditor using the procedure for that creditor along with the **"creditor's agreement to clear collec-**

tion account" letter. Follow the same logic of Step **1a** but include the logic of the **"debt schedule" settlement letter**. You are offering to repay the money according to a strict schedule; you are asking to have your credit cleared, the repayment terms extended, and, possibly, to have the debt reduced. Settlements of seventy cents on the dollar are common, but settlements as low as thirty cents on the dollar are possible. Offers of full payment will expedite the process.

2. If the collection account is already paid: you should dispute the item through the credit bureaus (see **Basic Dispute**). Because you don't owe any money that they want, you don't have any leverage with the collection agency. There are many reasons why an account could be put into collection improperly. Maybe you weren't billed at the right address, or maybe the creditor ignored your requests for clarification of a bill (see **Fair Credit Billing Act**).

3. Follow up the settlement letter with a letter to the credit bureaus (see **Advanced Credit Bureau Dispute: Documentation Letter**) to make sure that they ultimately remove the derogatory items you have negotiated off with the creditors.

Notes on Collection Agency Negotiations

Don't admit to any wrongdoing, don't merely pay, and don't be threatened. You want your the trail of bad credit cleared in exchange for settling the debt. You have leverage because:

- They want the money.
- You can control the way in which they contact you (see **Fair Debt Practices Collection Act**).
- You can refuse to deal with the collection agency (see **cease communication letter**), which as a matter of course causes the debt to revert back to the original creditor.

The first rule of dealing with collection agencies is *don't be intimi-dated*. They will often threaten to ruin your credit, not to mention your life. The law, however, regulates what they can and can't do (see **Fair Debt Collection Practices Act**).

Finally, unless your original agreement with the creditor provided for special collection fees, the collection agency cannot tack on extra fees for their "service." Don't fall for this common trick.

Creditor Type: Public Records

PUBLIC RECORDS BACKGROUND

Any conviction, court suit, judgment, or tax lien is a matter of public record that may be picked up and reported by the credit bureaus.

Even if you believe that the suit or judgment is unjustified, and can get the other side of the case to agree with you, the credit bureaus have taken the position that what occurred, how-ever unjustified, is history, and therefore in the realm of their reporting.

The credit bureaus collect public records in huge gulps of electronic data gathered by subcontractors who compile the re-cords for sale. These companies are notorious for their care-lessness. In one celebrated instance, the taxpayers of an entire Vermont town were reported as having tax liens. The shoddy means by which public records are compiled are equaled only by the quality of credit bureau efforts to verify the information when challenged. Much to the dismay of lenders and other people who depend on credit reports, credit bureaus sometimes don't even bother to confirm information that is disputed even when sub-stantiation is readily available.

PUBLIC RECORDS STRATEGY

The two dispute paths depend on whether or not you actually owe money.

If the derogatory public record involves a situation where you owe money, you can try to cut a deal with the creditor or creditor's attorney.

In order to vacate a judgment, you will likely need the help of an attorney (see **Appendix VII: Using a Lawyer**), especially if you are facing a collection attorney. A thorough collection attorney can eventually get a marshal to enforce collection of the debt. This can involve seizure and sale of your worldly possessions.

If you still owe the money on a judgment filed by a private individual or concern, you might persuade the opposing attorney to vacate the judgment in exchange for payment. Do not confuse this with satisfying the judgment, which only means that you paid when you were forced to. Vacating the judgment means that the judgment has been found defective in some way or that, at least, the opposition feels that the judgment is sufficiently unenforceable that they are willing to settle the matter rather than further pursue the issue with you in court.

Judges have shown a dislike for vacating judgments that were made based on the facts. They are more comfortable with having them satisfied. Still, your attorney can work to have the opposing attorney see the wisdom of accepting payment in exchange for a letter that shows her willingness to have the judgment vacated. The phrase "this judgment may be vacated without prior notice by either party" may be useful to your lawyer in the settlement. The written settlement should always be sent to the credit bureaus (see **Advanced Credit Bureau Dispute: Documentation Letter**) to make sure that they remove the item.

If the derogatory public record in dispute is not current, your best bet is to work through the credit bureaus. When conducting your **basic** dispute, keep in mind that public records that don't come off in the first round often come off in the second.

Notes on Verbal Negotiations

Creditors are generally aggressive, demeaning, and capable of doing and saying anything to get you to pay. Respect has little to do with their job. Fortunately for you, the law generally gives a second chance to pay up, and creditors are restrained to some extent from unfair debt collection practices. In reality, though, creditors lie, abuse, badger, and cheat to get paid. Professional credit departments for most credit-granting organizations are staffed with individuals who are trained with finely honed rhetorical weapons, designed to instill the guilt and fear that will motivate payment.

Don't make your arguments personal. Focus on the facts of your case, and never get angry at the person representing the other side. Say, "I know you're just doing your job." The person you're dealing with is likely following policy, and to the limited extent that they can influence policy, you are best placed in their good graces. Many, many credit situations involve the person on the other side deciding on his or her own discretion to give you some slack. This is a prime consideration when calling on the phone to get bad credit removed. Statements that are likely to help:

> "I realized that this isn't your doing, and that you have a job with responsibilities. Here's the problem. The bad credit mark from your company that is on my credit report is the only thing that is stopping the mortgage from going through (the baby from getting a crib; my mother from having a last vacation . . . she's very sick, you know). Could you please, please, please help me with this. I'm a paying customer, and I'm going to continue doing business with you, so please help out here."

The person you are dealing with is elevated, and the problem is reduced to the basic life issues. Your position is easy to understand and easy to go along with.

Avoid ultimatums. Instead of saying, "I want you to fix my credit—or else," try: "I am interested in resolving the credit problem and I need your help. I will satisfy you in whatever reasonable manner necessary to get this problem resolved."

You might offer up some possible reasons why the item was not really late, or that there was a misunderstanding. They might be willing to offer a payment schedule in exchange for clearing the credit. If there were irregularities, or if you can express your claim of problems in a convincing manner, they may just go along with you whether they agree with your claims or not.

The **Fair Credit Billing Act** and the **Fair Credit Reporting Act** have provisions that detail the rules for what is an on-time payment and what is a correct billing procedure. The existence of billing errors, which would mean you weren't really late, will allow the creditor, that is, the creditor's agent in the collections department, to erase the credit.

These requirements for proper billing can be used to shift the burden of proof to the creditor. The other side will, in many instances, cave in rather than fight, whether they believe you or not.

An example of an error we've seen claimed that resulted in the clearing of credit is:

> "The bills were sent to my address while construction work was going on. We requested that the bills be sent to my job. It was only after the work was done and we moved back home that we found your bill. Of course we paid when we knew about it."

This tactic, executed as good-natured cajoling, goes a long way in the credit reporting world, especially if the past-due accounts have been brought up to date, or the latenesses are older.

If the other side still won't budge: You must offer a number of options on how the problem can be resolved, including a plan the creditor may have in mind, and then choose one.

Offering several possible solutions allows both sides to bring more to the table than was originally in discussion. For example, the original creditor requests that you start making payments to bring the account at least out of collection. This request could be negotiated by you to a larger initial payment, and the promise of accelerated paydown of the debt in exchange for cleared credit.

When you negotiate a payment plan, admit no guilt, and assign no blame to the other party. Just stick to the misunderstanding ("The bills weren't coming to me because of construction, I notified you. We obviously didn't communicate well with each other, but I'd like to rectify this now by paying you. Please don't penalize me by ruining my credit.")

When dealing with credit departments, keep it real. Don't insult anyone's intelligence with outlandish fakery. Keep it simple and stick to your explanation. Again your goal is to get your credit cleared.

Don't give up. Often, repetitive claims of a misunderstanding coupled with your willingness to pay, driven home to each successive layer of entrenched bureaucracy in the credit department, all the way from the customer-service rep to the supervisor to the manager to the manager's vice-president, gets the job done.

In moving from customer-service rep up the line to the vice-president, remember to focus on the problem, not pick on the people:

> "I understand it's your job to say no to people like me when the issues are not cut-and-dry. You must understand that—except for this misunderstanding, which I've tried to explain—I pay my accounts, and I can't accept no for an answer. Please, may I speak to a supervisor. By the way, what's your name? I wanted to thank you for listening to my problem, even if you couldn't help out. And what's your supervisor's name? Do they have a direct-dial number over there just in case we get cut off?"

Listen to the person's tone. In credit departments, especially in better-managed companies, the first layer of customer service is supposed to take care of the problem. If they can't, it reflects poorly on them. The higher you go, the more poorly it reflects on the lower levels of customer service.

The negotiation is going your way when someone answers your request to speak to the next level with a strained, "I don't know what good it will do you." In general, moving up the ladder means overcoming obstacles to success. The more strain this request causes, the more likely you will succeed at the next level. When the strain is palpable, repeat some formulation of your original offer to pay, or maybe even your willingness to just go away if you've already paid, in exchange for clear credit. Restate the original misunderstanding in human terms.

Get agreements *in writing*. Most companies will send you a letter verifying that they are correcting the credit and notifying the credit bureaus. You'll need this letter for your own disputes with the credit bureaus (see **Advanced Credit Bureau Dispute: Documentation Letter**), in addition to securing your agreement with the creditor.

Advanced: Full Factual Glossing

In the preparation of a mortgage application, a minimum of two credit-bureau reports are combined as the basis of what is known as a **Full Factual Credit Report**, or a Residential Mortgage Report. These reports are prepared by a number of credit-reporting companies that are essentially subcontractors to the three major credit bureaus. They function as service companies to the mortgage industry.

For a fee of around fifty dollars, these mortgage-reporting companies go beyond the work of a credit bureau and actually make phone calls (among other verification methods) to make a more informed judgment about your creditworthiness. They verify your employment, salary, address, and—here's the good part—are obligated to issue a corrected credit report if you provide them with evidence of errors in your credit history. The advantage is that the corrected report is issued in days, not the weeks and months that the credit bureaus can take. The disadvantage is that the corrections are not disseminated nationally, so you still have to go through a repair process with the credit bureaus.

This is really only useful if you're applying for a mortgage. Unfortunately, credit bureaus and nearly all non–mortgage lenders will only rarely accept a clean Full Factual Credit Report (or any outside documentation) as a basis for removing derogatory items. The shame is that the Full Factual Credit Report is the only report in the credit-reporting business that allows for your corrections to be quickly investigated and processed.

HOW TO

If you apply for a mortgage, the mortgage broker or lending institution will take down basic financial and personal information, which they will then forward to a full factual mortgage-reporting company (essentially a small credit bureau) to investigate your creditworthiness.

If there are any derogatory items in your credit reports, you'll get a letter from your potential lender asking you to verify their accuracy and explain the circumstances of them.

You can wait for this letter or you can save two weeks by anticipating it. When the mortgage-reporting company opens its investigations, it assigns your case a control number. Once you have this number—you can get it from the mortgage broker or would-be lender—you can communicate directly with the investigating company to dispute derogatory items in your credit history. If this number is not available, you can provide your dispute information to the broker to be forwarded to the investigating company.

You should be as simple as possible in your disputes, relying on straightforward explanations and/or supporting documents (i.e., bills, canceled checks, receipts). Follow the format of the **initial dispute letter** used for the credit bureaus. This process is set up to quickly correct errors that would kill a mortgage deal, and it takes place on a more personal level than your typical disputes with the credit bureaus.

Sometimes a full factual reporting agency will take the position that disputes should only be conducted with the major credit bureaus, but under the law (see **FCRA**), they are a "credit-reporting agency" with the same responsibilities as a credit bureau. You may need to firmly remind a supervisor of this fact when asking the full factual agency to fix errors.

Full factual glossing is often reserved for speedy follow-up to negotiated settlements of credit disputes. A typical example would be cutting a deal with a creditor: "I'll pay you what I owe—if you give me a clean record of payment."

Creditor's "Restrictively Endorsed" Settlement Letter

This method uses what's known as a restrictively endorsed payment and a return receipt to create a legal agreement between you and a creditor. Your terms become an agreement when the creditor cashes your check. Even if the creditor doesn't honor your call for clearing your credit, the credit bureaus must and do (see **Advanced Credit Bureau Dispute: Documentation Letter**).

Some creditors, such as mortgage lenders, will not accept restrictively endorsed payment instruments. *With that said, unscrupulous people have sent restrictive endorsement agreements to the credit bureaus claiming that they were sent to creditors with payment.*

The restrictively endorsed payment can be combined with a **"debt schedule" settlement letter**.

creditor name
*creditor address**
creditor phone

date

Dear Customer Service:

Enclosed please find payment for my charge account. Your acceptance of the check signifies that the account is *[paid in full or paid up to date]* and that you will delete all derogatory items with all the major credit bureaus.

Thank you. I want to extend my thanks to the customer service department for being so helpful with this misunderstanding.

Yours truly,
J. Q. Public

Remember when using this letter, and all letters in this book, to:

1. Reword the letter in your own words. You don't want to appear like you are being coached or following a repair strategy.
2. Keep a photocopy of the letter for your records. The copies are often used later on in the repair process.
3. Send the letter through *certified/return receipt* mail. This is proof that you sent the letter.

---

*Creditor address: It is important to use the correct address on the bill. Although there may be more than one address, the one on the back of the bill is the one you should use.

"Creditor's Agreement to Clear Collection Account" Letter

This letter is useful for creditors who do not report to credit bureaus, but who refer past-due accounts to collection agencies. The collection agencies, it should come as no surprise, are active credit bureau reporters (see **Creditor Type: Collection Agencies** for more detail).

The purpose of the letter is to get the creditor to call off the collection agency. If you do not do it correctly, the collection agency will merely report your late account as PAID COLLECTION ACCOUNT, which is still a bad mark on your credit report.

You don't need this letter if the collection agency agrees to clear the bad credit, but that is ordinarily more difficult to achieve than getting a creditor to agree to this letter. Many small-time creditors like doctors or a local hardware stores are surprised when they find how unhelpful their collection agencies are, and you sometimes have to open their eyes to the problem. This letter gets it in writing so that even if the creditor doesn't follow through, you still have proof of the agreement for the credit bureaus (see **Advanced Credit Bureau Dispute: Documentation Letter**).

The word "misunderstanding" is an effective way to characterize the collection situation without admitting or assigning blame.

The agreement can be combined with a **"debt schedule"** **settlement letter**.

creditor name
*creditor address**
creditor phone

date

Dear *[use the contact's name]*:

I am glad that we are able to settle our misunder-standing. Enclosed please find *[full, or if you're are using a repayment schedule, the first installment]* payment. Your acceptance of the check signifies that the account is *[paid in full or paid up to date]* and that you will contact the relevant credit bureaus and collection agencies to delete any collection accounts or other derogatory credit.

I appreciate your cooperation and service. Thank you.

Best regards,
J. Q. Public

Remember when using this letter, and all letters in this book, to:

1. Reword the letter in your own words. You don't want to appear like you are being coached or following a repair strategy.
2. Keep a photocopy of the letter for your records. The copies are often used later on in the repair process.
3. Send the letter through *certified/return receipt* mail. This is proof that you sent the letter.

*Creditor address: It is important to use the correct address on the bill. Though there may be more than one address, the one on the back of the bill is the one you should use.

Creditor "Debt Schedule" Settlement Letter

Use this letter (or a variation, depending on your circumstances) when you negotiate to repay a debt through regular payments. The repayment terms can vary widely, but the basic point is that you want your credit cleared as soon as you start paying the money back.

Lump sums are the most likely to induce a creditor to accept your offer of partial payment. Still, since debt counselors commonly use 40-month repayment plans and Chapter 13 bankruptcy often involves 60-month repayment plans, an offer of payment in 12 to 24 months will be relatively fast. Keeping the plan under a year is the next best thing to a lump sum.

Remember when using this letter, and all letters in this book, to:

1. Reword the letter in your own words. You don't want to appear like you are being coached or following a repair strategy.
2. Keep a photocopy of the letter for your records. The copies are often used later on in the repair process.
3. Send the letter through *certified/return receipt* mail. This is proof that you sent the letter.

creditor name
*creditor address**
creditor phone

date

Dear Customer Service:

Due to severe financial and health problems in my family, I find it necessary to settle my debts as best I can.

With this letter, I offer to settle my outstanding debt to you for 30% of its total amount. In other words, I am offering you $_____$ to be paid in _____ monthly payments of $_____$. As long as I stick to these payment terms, you agree to delete all derogatory credit and report this account as current and satisfactory.

If this is agreeable to you, please sign and date below and return to me.

Thank you. I want to extend my thanks to the customer service department for being so helpful with this misunderstanding.

Yours truly,   _____
J. Q. Public   *creditor name and date*

*Creditor address: It is important to use the correct address on the bill. Though there may be more than one address, the one on the back of the bill is the one you should use.

Student Loan "Forbearance Notification" Letter

Student loans that leave repayment until after graduation require the borrower to notify all lenders about school enrollment or other circumstances that allow a forbearance on repayment of the loan. If the lender pushes your loan into default, you will want to show the credit bureaus that you served lender with a forbearance letter (see **Advanced Credit Bureau Dispute: Documentation Letter**).

Remember when using this letter, and all letters in this book, to:

1. Reword the letter in your own words. You don't want to appear like you are being coached or following a repair strategy.
2. Keep a photocopy of the letter for your records. The copies are often used later on in the repair process.
3. Send the letter through *certified/return receipt* mail. This is proof that you sent the letter.

student loan lender name
*student loan lender address**
student loan lender phone

date

Dear Customer Service:

Please consider this formal notification that I am still in school, and therefore the terms of the forbearance of my student loan are still in effect. I will notify you when I have graduated—and the subsequent grace period has elapsed—by sending you a check for the first payment on my loan.

Thank you.

Yours truly,
J. Q. Public

---

*Student loan lender address: It is important to use the correct address, which you will find on the loan agreement itself. Many lenders have more than one address, and use a different address for each of their various loan products.

Advanced Credit Bureau Dispute: Documentation Letter

Use this letter as a follow-up to an unresolved dispute with a creditor. Its purpose is to prompt the credit bureau to remove derogatory items that the creditor may not have corrected. You can send any documentation with this letter—the more the better—but the following settlement letters are especially effective because they substantiate an agreement between you and the creditor: **"Restrictively endorsed," "debt schedule,"** and **student loan "forbearance notification"** letters. Also include, with all documentation, photocopies of postal return receipts and canceled checks whenever possible. It is unethical to send copies of the above letters to credit bureaus that you never actually sent to creditors, but anecdotal evidence suggests that credit bureaus don't generally investigate the validity of consumer-supplied documentation.

Remember when using this letter, and all letters in this book, to:

1. Reword the letter in your own words. You don't want to appear like you are being coached or following a repair strategy.
2. Keep a photocopy of the letter for your records. The copies are often used later on in the repair process.
3. Send the letter through *certified/return receipt* mail. This is proof that you sent the letter.

creditor name
*creditor address**
creditor phone

date

Dear Customer Service:

The following error is still on my report despite the fact that I have documentation (enclosed) that demonstrates that this should no longer be reported as bad credit. I would not press such a minor matter if the consequences weren't so severe. I stand to lose money if this is not corrected posthaste.

LONE STAR BANK CORP account number 4483847293472394.

The enclosed documentation proves that this should be corrected to reflect my good credit.

Yours,
Joy Q. Public

*Creditor address: It is important to use the correct address on the bill. Though there may be more than one address, the one on the back of the bill is the one you should use.

Revolving Credit: Billing Clarification Letter

Many of your rights as a revolving credit borrower derive from the Fair Credit Billing Act (see **Appendix V**). Revolving credit is the technical name for a credit card or department store account. It revolves because you can borrow and pay on a monthly basis, with a credit ceiling and a minimum payment. It is distinguished from an installment loan (typically a mortgage, student, or car loan) that has a predetermined monthly payment.

This letter sets the stage for invoking some of your most robust rights under the Fair Credit Billing Act. The act requires revolving credit lenders to bill you accurately, and at the address that you state, on a monthly basis.

This means that your payment is not late if, within two billing cycles, you send in a request for clarification of amounts due. Under the Fair Billing Act, this request for clarification is classified as a billing error. The payment cannot, therefore, be reported as "late."

With return receipt proof of having mailed this clarification letter, you can demand that affected lateness on your credit report be corrected. Even without return receipt proof, sending a copy of the letter is often enough to get either the creditor or credit bureau to correct latenesses (see **Advanced Credit Bureau Dispute: Documentation Letter**).

Remember when using this letter, and all letters in this book, to:

1. Reword the letter in your own words. You don't want to appear like you are being coached or following a repair strategy.
2. Keep a photocopy of the letter for your records. The copies are often used later on in the repair process.
3. Send the letter through *certified/return receipt mail*. This is proof that you sent the letter.

creditor name
creditor address*
creditor phone

date

Dear Customer Service:

On my latest bill *[be specific about card number and billing date]*, I am confused by the amount owing. I am not sure if one of the charges is correct. *[List the charge.]*

Since I am writing you within two billing cycles of the actual charge, I request that you not report this specific payment as late.

Thank you. I want to extend my thanks to the customer service department for being so helpful with this misunderstanding.

Yours truly,
J. Q. Public

---

*Creditor address: It is important to use the correct address on the bill. Though there may be more than one address, the one on the back of the bill is the one you should use.

Revolving Credit: Change of Billing Address Letter

Many of your rights as a revolving credit borrower derive from the Fair Credit Billing Act (see page 141). Revolving credit is the technical name for a credit card or department store account. It revolves because you can borrow and pay on a monthly basis, with a credit ceiling and a minimum payment. It is distinguished from an installment loan (typically a mortgage, student, or car loan) that has a predetermined monthly payment.

This letter sets the stage for invoking some of your most robust rights under the Fair Credit Billing Act. The act requires revolving credit lenders to bill you accurately, and at the address that you state, on a monthly basis.

This means that ten days before the end of any billing cycle, you can change your billing address. If the creditor does not bill you at the new address that you specify, then you haven't been billed and you therefore can't be late with payment.

(You can also use the "change of address form" if one came with the bill. You can always send in a blank copy of the same form as evidence that you earlier sent in a completed form.)

With return receipt proof of having mailed this change of address letter, you can demand that affected latenesses on your credit report be corrected. Even without return receipt proof, sending a copy of such a letter is often enough to get either the creditor or credit bureau to correct latenesses (see **Advanced Credit Bureau Dispute: Documentation Letter**).

Customer service departments will often counter the exercise of your Fair Credit Billing Act rights with specious arguments, such as: "If you charged it, you should have known about it"; "We don't have to bill you, it's just a courtesy"; "The bill wasn't returned, so it must have been received." Don't be intimidated by these arguments.

---

creditor name
creditor address*
creditor phone

date

Dear Customer Service:

Consider this letter formal notice of a change in my billing address for my account with you *[be specific about card number]*.

Thank you. I am a satisfied and loyal customer.

Yours truly,
J. Q. Public

Remember when using this letter, and all letters in this book, to:

1. Reword the letter in your own words. You don't want to appear like you are being coached or following a repair strategy.
2. Keep a photocopy of the letter for your records. The copies are often used later on in the repair process.
3. Send the letter through *certified/return receipt mail*. This is proof that you sent the letter.

---

*Creditor address: It is important to use the correct address on the bill. Though there may be more than one address; the one on the back of the bill is the one you should use.

Advanced Credit Repair: Sample Explanation Letter

The Fair Credit Reporting Act requires the credit bureaus to include, at your request, a statement from you of up to 100 words explaining each and any derogatory credit item that was satisfactorily resolved in a dispute (see the **Annotated FCRA**).

This is a last-ditch technique, after you've given up. It's not really a repair tactic, because it doesn't improve your credit. Nevertheless, in hopeless cases such as car repossessions, it's still better than nothing. Just the fact that you bothered to include an explanation can demonstrate a certain reliability on your part.

In composing your explanation, do not assign blame. Show how you have taken responsibility for your life and the problems you faced. This sample concerns a "voluntary surrender" item listed on a car loan.

Remember when using this letter, and all letters in this book, to:

1. Reword the letter in your own words. You don't want to appear like you are being coached or following a repair strategy.
2. Keep a photocopy of the letter for your records. The copies are often used later on in the repair process.
3. Send the letter through *certified/return receipt* mail. This is proof that you sent the letter.

credit bureau name
*credit bureau address**

date

Dear Sir or Madam:

Please append the explanation below to my credit report with regard to the following account:

Ford Credit 23456789.

At the end of 1989, downsizing in my industry led to massive layoffs. When I lost my job, I could not continue making car payments so I voluntarily surrendered the car.

I took the layoff as an opportunity to be retrained for the position I now have with my present employer. Now that I am working again, I am pleased to be current with all my credit accounts. Credit is very important to me; I regard it as keeping my word.

Thank you. Please send me a copy of the amended credit report.

Yours truly,
J. Q. Public

---

*Collection agency address: It is important to use the correct address on the notice.

Advanced Credit Repair: Cease Communication Letter

This letter is useful if a collection agency won't negotiate or accept a restrictively endorsed payment. After receiving the letter, the collection agency is allowed only one last chance to contact you, and then only to tell you what will happen next.

In effect, this letter cuts the collection agency off at the knees. The agency may return the debt to the original creditor, who should be more willing to negotiate, but you can still call up the collection agency and press your offer one last time before the collection agency gives up the debt (and chance to profit).

Remember when using this letter, and all letters in this book, to:

1. Reword the letter in your own words. You don't want to appear like you are being coached or following a repair strategy.
2. Keep a photocopy of the letter for your records. The copies are often used later on in the repair process.
3. Send the letter through *certified/return receipt mail*. This is proof that you sent the letter.

collection agency name
*collection agency address**

date

Dear Sir or Madam:

Please cease communication with me in regard to *creditor name, account numbers, and debt*. If you do not abide by this request, you will be in violation of the Fair Debt Collection Practices Act.

Yours truly,
J. Q. Public

---

*Collection agency address: It is important to use the correct address on the notice.

Appendixes

I. Credit Bureau and FTC Addresses

II. Cost of Consumer Credit Reports

III. Fair Credit Reporting Act

IV. Fair Debt Collection Practices

V. Fair Credit Billing Act

VI. Truth in Lending Act

VII. Using a Lawyer

Appendix I

CREDIT BUREAU AND FTC ADDRESSES

The super-bureaus have many mailing addresses, but at press time these addresses listed below are the ones to use for your initial letters. They shouldn't set off any alarms at the credit bureaus.

You may want to make a free call to the 800 information operator (1-800/555-1212) and confirm that the phone numbers and addresses have not changed.

In their responses the credit bureaus may direct you to send future letters to a regional office. You should use the regional addresses when you get them. Don't be confused if the regional office uses a variation on the credit bureau's name or an entirely different name. TRW's regional office in Hawaii, for example, is called Credit Data of Hawaii.

> Equifax Information Service
> Customer Correspondence
> P.O. Box 740193
> Atlanta, GA 30374-0193
> (800) 685-1111

TRW
12606 Greenville Avenue
P.O. Box 749-029
Dallas, TX 75374
(800) 392-1122

TransUnion
P.O. Box 8070
North Olmsted, OH 44070-8070
(800) 922-5490

Federal Trade Commission (FTC)
attention: Credit Bureau Complaints
Pennsylvania Avenue & 6th St. N.W.
Washington, DC 20580

Appendix II

COST OF CONSUMER CREDIT REPORTS

The cost of a credit report will probably not match these prices exactly. You should contact the credit bureaus by 800 number to confirm the addresses (see Appendix I) and charges. Some states, such as Maine, regulate the cost of credit reports.

TRW	first report for free, second report for $7.50
TransUnion	$8 per report
Equifax	$8 per report

Important: Add your local sales tax to the above prices.

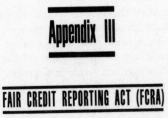

Appendix III

FAIR CREDIT REPORTING ACT (FCRA)

The FCRA provides the basic tools for credit repair. It is badly in need of updating to regulate the credit bureaus; in the absence of reform from Congress, most progress has been made by state attorneys general in court. The repair section makes extensive use of the act, but it may help to read the actual law, included here in full for you.

TITLE VI—PROVISIONS RELATING TO CREDIT REPORTING AGENCIES

Amendment of Consumer Credit Protection Act

Sec. 601. The Consumer Credit Protection Act is amended by adding at the end thereof the following new title:

"TITLE VI—CONSUMER CREDIT REPORTING

"Sec. 601. Short title

"This title may be cited as the Fair Credit Reporting Act.

"Sec. 602. Findings and purpose

"(a) The Congress makes the following findings:

"(1) The banking system is dependent upon fair and accurate credit reporting. Inaccurate credit reports directly impair the efficiency of the banking system, and unfair credit reporting methods undermine the public confidence which is essential to the continued functioning of the banking system.

"(2) An elaborate mechanism has been developed for investigating and evaluating the credit worthiness, credit standing, credit capacity, character, and general reputation of consumers.

"(3) Consumer reporting agencies have assumed a vital role in assembling and evaluating consumer credit and other information on consumers.

"(4) There is a need to insure that consumer reporting agencies exercise their grave responsibilities with fairness, impartiality and a respect for the consumer's right to privacy.

"(b) It is the purpose of this title to require that consumer reporting agencies adopt reasonable procedures for meeting the needs of commerce for consumer credit, personnel, insurance, and other information in a manner which is fair and equitable to the consumer, with regard to the confidentially, accuracy, relevancy and proper utilization of such information in accordance with the requirements of this title.

"Sec. 603. Definitions and rules of construction

"(a) Definitions and rules of construction set forth in this section are applicable for the purposes of this title.

"(b) The term 'person' means any individual, partnership, corporation, trust, estate, cooperative, association, government or governmental subdivision or agency, or other entity.

"(c) The term 'consumer' means an individual.

"(d) The term 'consumer report' means any written, oral, or other communication of any information by a consumer reporting agency bearing on a consumer's credit worthiness, credit standing, credit capacity, character, general reputation, personal characteristics, or mode of living which is used or expected to be used or collected in whole or in part for the purpose of serving as a factor in establishing the consumer's eligibility for (1) credit or insurance to be used primarily for personal, family, or household purposes, or (2) employment purposes, or (3) other purposes authorized under section 604. The term does not include (A) any report containing information solely as to transactions or experiences between the consumer and the person making the report; (B) any authorization or approval of a specific extension of credit directly or indirectly by the issuer of a credit card or similar device; or (C) any report in which a person who has been requested by a third party to make a specific extension of credit directly or indirectly to a consumer conveys his decision with respect to such request, if the third party advises the consumer of the name and address of the person to whom the request was made and such person makes the disclosures to the consumer required under section 615.

"(e) The term 'investigative consumer report' means a consumer report or portion thereof in which information on a consumer's character, general reputation, personal characteristics, or mode of living is obtained through personal interviews with neighbors, friends, or associates of the consumer reported on or with others with whom he is acquainted or who may have knowledge concerning any such items of information. However, such information shall not include specific factual information on a consumer's credit record obtained directly from a creditor of the consumer or from a consumer reporting agency when such information was obtained directly from a creditor of the consumer or from the consumer.

"(f) The term 'consumer reporting agency' means any person which, for monetary fees, dues, or on a cooperative nonprofit basis, regularly engages in whole or in part in the practice of assembling or evaluating consumer credit information or other information on consumers for the purpose of furnishing consumer reports to third parties, and which uses any means or facility of interstate commerce for the purpose of preparing or furnishing consumer reports.

"(g) The term 'file' when used in connection with information on any consumer, means all of the information on that consumer recorded and retained by a consumer reporting agency regardless of how the information is stored.

"(h) The term 'employment purposes' when used in connection with a consumer report means a report used for the purpose of evaluating a consumer for employment, promotion, reassignment, or retention as an employee.

"(i) The term 'medical information' means information or records obtained, with the consent of the individual to whom it relates, from licensed physicians or medical practitioners, hospitals, clinics, or other medical or medically related facilities.

"Sec. 604. Permissible purposes of reports

"A consumer reporting agency may furnish a consumer report under the following circumstances and no other:

"(1) In response to the order of a court having jurisdiction to issue such an order.

"(2) In accordance with the written instructions of the consumer to whom it relates.

"(3) To a person which it has reason to believe—

"(A) intends to use the information in connection with a credit transaction involving the consumer on whom the information is to be furnished and involving the extension of credit to, or review or collection of an account of, the consumer; or

"(B) intends to use the information for employment purposes; or

"(C) intends to use the information in connection with the underwriting of insurance involving the consumer; or

"(D) intends to use the information in connection with a determination of the consumer's eligibility for a license or other benefit granted by a governmental instrumentality required by law to consider an applicant's financial responsibility or status; or

"(E) otherwise has a legitimate business need for the information in connection with a business transaction involving the consumer.

"Sec. 605. Obsolete information

"(a) Except as authorized under subsection (b), no consumer reporting agency may make any consumer report containing any of the following items of information:

"(1) Cases under title 11 of the United States Code or under the Bankruptcy Act that, from the date of entry of the order for relief or the date of adjudication, as the cause may be, antedate the report by more than 10 years.

"(2) Suits and judgments which, from date of entry, antedate the report by more than seven years or until the governing statute of limitations has expired, whichever is the longer period.

"(3) Paid tax liens which, from date of payment, antedate the report by more than seven years.

"(4) Accounts placed for collection or charged to profit and loss which antedate the report by more than seven years.

"(5) Records of arrest, indictment, or conviction of crime which, from date of disposition, release, or parole, antedate the report by more than seven years.

"(6) Any other adverse item of information which antedates the report by more than seven years.

"(b) The provisions of subsection (a) are not applicable in the case of any consumer credit report to be used in connection with—

"(1) a credit transaction involving, or which may reasonably be expected to involve, a principal amount of $50,000 or more;

"(2) the underwriting of life insurance involving, or which may reasonably be expected to involve, a face amount of $50,000 or more; or

"(3) the employment of any individual at an annual salary which equals, or which may reasonably be expected to equal $20,000, or more.

"Sec. 606. Disclosure of investigative consumer reports

"(a) A person may not procure or cause to be prepared an investigative consumer report on any consumer unless—

"(1) it is clearly and accurately disclosed to the consumer that an investigative consumer report including information as to his character, general reputation, personal characteristics, and mode of living, whichever are applicable, may be made, and such disclosure (A) is made in a writing mailed, or otherwise delivered, to the consumer, not later than three days after the date on which the report was first requested, and (B) includes a statement informing the consumer of his right to request the additional disclosures provided for under subsection (b) of this section; or

"(2) the report is to be used for employment purposes for which the consumer has not specifically applied.

"(b) Any person who procures or causes to be prepared an investigative consumer report on any consumer shall, upon written request made by the consumer within a reasonable period of time after the receipt by him of the disclosure required by subsection (a) (1), make a complete and accurate disclosure of the nature and scope of the investigation requested. This disclosure shall be made in a writing mailed, or otherwise delivered, to the consumer not later than five days after the date on which the request for such disclosure was received from the consumer or such report was first requested, whichever is the later.

"(c) No person may be held liable for any violation of subsection (a) or (b) of this section if he shows by a preponderance of the evidence that at the time of the violation he maintained reasonable procedures to assure compliance with subsection (a) or (b).

"Sec. 607. Compliance procedures

"(a) Every consumer reporting agency shall maintain reasonable procedures designed to avoid violations of section 605 and to limit the furnishing of consumer reports to the purposes listed under section 604. These procedures shall require that prospective users of the information identify themselves, certify the purposes for which the information is sought, and certify that the information will be used for no other purpose. Every consumer reporting agency shall make a reasonable effort to verify the identity of a new prospective user and the uses certified by such prospective user prior to furnishing such user a consumer report. No consumer reporting agency may furnish a consumer report to any person if it has reasonable grounds for believing that the consumer report will not be used for a purpose listed in section 604.

"(b) Whenever a consumer reporting agency prepares a consumer report it shall follow reasonable procedures to assure maximum possible accuracy of the information concerning the individual about whom the report relates.

"Sec. 608. Disclosures to governmental agencies

"Notwithstanding the provisions of section 604, a consumer reporting agency may furnish identifying information respecting any consumer, limited to his name, address, former addresses, places of employment, or former places of employment, to a governmental agency.

"Sec. 609. Disclosures to consumers

"(a) Every consumer reporting agency shall, upon request and proper identification of any consumer, clearly and accurately disclose to the consumer:

"(1) The nature and substance of all information (except medical information) in its files on the consumer at the time of the request.

"(2) The sources of the information; except that the sources of information acquired solely for use in preparing an investigative consumer report and actually used for no other purpose need not be disclosed. Provided, That in the event an action is brought under this title, such sources shall be available to the plaintiff under appropriate discovery procedures in the court in which the action is brought.

"(3) The recipients of any consumer report on the consumer which it has furnished—

"(A) for employment purposes within the two-year period preceding the request, and

"(B) for any other purpose within the six-month period preceding the request.

"(b) The requirements of subsection (a) respecting the disclosure of sources of information and the recipients of consumer reports do not apply to information received or consumer reports furnished prior to the effective date of this title except to the extent that the matter involved is contained in the files of the consumer reporting agency on that date.

"Sec. 610. Conditions of disclosure to consumers

"(a) A consumer reporting agency shall make the disclosures required under section 609 during normal business hours and on reasonable notice.

"(b) The disclosures required under section 609 shall be made to the consumer—

"(1) in person if he appears in person and furnishes proper identification; or

"(2) by telephone if he has made a written request, with proper identification, for telephone disclosure and the toll charge, if any, for the telephone call is prepaid by or charged directly to the consumer.

"(c) Any consumer reporting agency shall provide trained personnel to explain to the consumer any information furnished to him pursuant to section 609.

"(d) The consumer shall be permitted to be accompanied by one other person of his choosing, who shall furnish reasonable identification. A consumer reporting agency may require the consumer to furnish a written statement granting permission to the consumer reporting agency to discuss the consumer's file in such person's presence.

"(e) Except as provided in sections 616 and 617, no consumer may bring any action or proceeding in the nature of defamation, invasion of privacy, or negligence with respect to the reporting of information against any consumer reporting agency, any user of information, or any person who furnishes information to a consumer reporting agency, based on information disclosed pursuant to section 609, 610, or 615, except as to false information furnished with malice or willful intent to injure such consumer.

"Sec. 611. Procedure in case of disputed accuracy

"(a) If the completeness or accuracy of any item of information contained in his file is disputed by a consumer, and such dispute is directly conveyed to the consumer reporting agency by the consumer, the consumer reporting agency shall within a reasonable period of time reinvestigate and record the current status of that information unless it has reasonable grounds to believe that the dispute by the consumer is frivolous or irrelevant. If after such reinvestigation such information is found to be inaccurate or can no longer be verified, the consumer reporting agency shall promptly delete such information. The presence of contradictory information in the consumer's file does not in and of itself constitute reasonable grounds for believing the dispute is frivolous or irrelevant.

"(b) If the reinvestigation does not resolve the dispute, the consumer may file a brief statement setting forth the nature of the dispute. The consumer reporting agency may limit such statements to not more than one hundred words if it provides the consumer with assistance in writing a clear summary of the dispute.

"(c) Whenever a statement of a dispute is filed, unless there is reasonable grounds to believe that it is frivolous or irrelevant, the consumer reporting agency shall, in any subsequent consumer report containing the information in question, clearly note that it is disputed by the consumer and provide either the consumer's statement or a clear and accurate codification or summary thereof.

"(d) Following any deletion of information which is found to be inaccurate or whose accuracy can no longer be verified or any notation as to disputed information, the consumer reporting agency shall, at the request of the consumer, furnish notification that the item has been deleted or the statement, codification, or summary pursuant to subsection (b) or (c) to any person specifically designated by the consumer who has within two years prior thereto received a consumer report for employment purposes, or within six months prior thereto received a consumer report for any other purpose, which contained the deleted or disputed information. The consumer reporting agency shall clearly and conspicuously disclose to the consumer his rights to make such a request. Such disclosure shall be made at or prior to the time the information is deleted or the consumer's statement regarding the disputed information is received.

"Sec. 612. Charges for certain disclosures

"A consumer reporting agency shall make all disclosures pursuant to section 609 and furnish all consumer reports pursuant to section 611 (d) without charge to the consumer if, within thirty days after receipt by such consumer of a notification pursuant to section 615 or notification from a debt collection agency affiliated with such consumer reporting agency stating that the consumer's credit rating may be or has been adversely affected, the consumer makes a request under section 609 or 611 (d). Otherwise, the consumer reporting agency may impose a reasonable charge on the consumer for making disclosure to such consumer pursuant to section 609, the charge for which shall be indicated to the consumer prior to making disclosure; and for furnishing notifications, statements, summaries, or codifications to person designated by the consumer pursuant to section 611 (d), the charge for which shall be indicated to the consumer prior to furnishing such information, and shall not exceed the charge that the consumer reporting agency would impose on each designated recipient for a consumer report except that no charge may be made for notifying such persons of the deletion of information which is found to be inaccurate or which can no longer be verified.

"Sec. 613. Public record information for employment purposes

"A consumer reporting agency which furnishes a consumer report for employment purposes and which for that purpose compiles and reports items of information on consumers which are matters of public record and are likely to have an adverse effect upon a consumer's ability to obtain employment shall—

"(1) at the time such public record information is reported to the user of such consumer report, notify the consumer of the fact that public record information is being reported by the consumer reporting agency, together with the name and address of the person to whom such information is being reported; or

"(2) maintain strict procedures designed to insure that whenever public record information which is likely to have an adverse effect on a consumer's ability to obtain employment is reported it is complete and up to date. For purposes of this paragraph, items of public record relating to arrest, indictments, convictions, suits, tax liens, and outstanding judgments shall be considered up to date if the current public record status of the item at the time of the report is reported.

"Sec. 614. Restrictions on investigative consumer reports

"Whenever a consumer reporting agency prepares an investigative consumer report, no adverse information in the consumer report (other than information which is a matter of public record) may be included in a subsequent consumer report unless such adverse information has been verified in the process of making such subsequent consumer report, or the adverse information was received within the three-month period preceding the date the subsequent report is furnished.

"Sec. 615. Requirements on users of consumer reports

"(a) Whenever credit or insurance for personal, family, or household purposes, or employment involving a consumer is denied or the charge for such credit or insurance is increased either wholly or partly because of information contained in a consumer report from a consumer reporting agency, the user of the consumer report shall so advise the consumer against whom such adverse action has been taken and supply the name and address of the consumer reporting agency making the report.

"(b) Whenever credit for personal, family, or household purposes involving a consumer is denied or the charge for such credit is increased either wholly or partly because of information obtained from a person other than a consumer reporting agency bearing upon the consumer's credit worthiness, credit standing, credit capacity, character, general reputation, personal characteristics, or mode of living, the user of such information shall, within a reasonable period of time, upon the consumer's written request for the reasons for such adverse action received within sixty days after learning of such adverse action, disclose the nature of the information to the consumer. The user of such information shall clearly and accurately disclose to the consumer his right to make such written requests at the time such adverse action is communicated to the consumer.

"(c) No person shall be held liable for any violation of this section if he shows by a preponderance of the evidence that at the time of the alleged violation he maintained reasonable procedures to assure compliance with the provisions of subsections (a) and (b).

"Sec. 616. Civil liability for willful noncompliance

"Any consumer reporting agency or user of information which willfully fails to comply with any requirement imposed under this title with respect to any consumer is liable to that consumer in an amount equal to the sum of—

"(1) any actual damages sustained by the consumer as a result of the failure;

"(2) such amount of punitive damages as the court may allow; and

"(3) in the case of any successful action to enforce any liability under this section, the costs of the action together with reasonable attorney's fees as determined by the court.

"Sec. 617. Civil liability for negligent noncompliance

"Any consumer reporting agency or user of information which is negligent in failing to comply with any requirement imposed under this title with respect to any consumer is liable to that consumer in an amount equal to the sum of—

"(1) any actual damages sustained by the consumer as a result of the failure;

"(2) in the case of any successful action to enforce any liability under this section, the costs of the action together with reasonable attorney's fees as determined by the court.

"Sec. 618. Jurisdiction of courts; limitation of actions

"An action to enforce any liability created under this title may be brought in any appropriate United States district court without regard to the amount in controversy, or in any other court of competent jurisdiction, within two years from the date on which the liability arises, except that where a defendant has materially and willfully misrepresented any information required under this title to be disclosed to an individual and the information so misrepresented is material to the establishment of the defendant's liability to that individual under this title, the action may be brought at any time within two years after discovery by the individual of the misrepresentation.

"Sec. 619. Obtaining information under false pretenses

"Any person who knowingly and willfully obtains information on a consumer from a consumer reporting agency under false pretense shall be fined not more than $5,000 or imprisoned not more than one year, or both.

"Sec. 620. Unauthorized disclosures by officers or employees

"Any officer or employee of a consumer reporting agency who knowingly and willfully provides information concerning an individual from the agency's files to a person not authorized to receive that information shall be fined not more than $5,000 or imprisoned not more than one year, or both.

"Sec. 621. Administrative enforcement

"(a) Compliance with the requirements imposed under this title shall be enforced under the Federal Trade Commission Act by the Federal Trade Commission with respect to consumer reporting agencies and all other persons subject thereto, except to the extent that enforcement of the requirements imposed under this title is specifically committed to some other government agency under subsection (b) hereof. For the purpose of the exercise by the Federal Trade Commission Act, a violation of any requirement or prohibition imposed under this title shall constitute an unfair or deceptive act or practice in commerce in violation of section 5 (a) of the Federal Trade Commission pursuant to this subsection, irrespective of whether that person is engaged in commerce or meets any other jurisdictional tests in the Federal Trade Commission Act. The Federal Trade Commission shall have such procedural, investigative, and enforcement powers, including the power to issue procedural rules in enforcing compliance with the requirements imposed under this title and to require the filing of reports, the production of documents, and the appearance of witnesses as though the applicable terms and conditions of the Federal Trade Commission Act were part of this title. Any person violating any of the provisions of this title shall be subject to the penalties and entitled to the privileges and immunities provided in the Federal Trade Commission Act as though the applicable terms and provisions thereof were part of this title.

"(b) Compliance with the requirements imposed under this title with respect to consumer reporting agencies and persons who use consumer reports from such agencies shall be enforced under—

"(1) section 8 of the Federal Deposit Insurance Act, in the case of:

"(A) national banks, by the Comptroller of the Currency;

"(B) member banks of the Federal Reserve Board; and

"(C) banks insured by the Federal Deposit Insurance Corporation (other than members of the Federal Reserve System), by the Board of Directors of the Federal Deposit Insurance Corporation.

"(2) section 5 (d) of the Home Owners Loan Act of 1933, section 407 of the National Housing Act, and sections 6 (i) and 17 of the Federal Home Loan Bank Act, by the Federal Home Loan Bank Board (acting directly or through the Federal Savings and Loan Insurance Corporation), in the case of any institution subject to any of those provisions;

"(3) the Federal Credit Union Act, by the Administrator of the National Credit Union Administration with respect to any Federal credit union;

"(4) the Acts to regulate commerce, by the Interstate Commerce Commission with respect to any common carrier subject to those Acts;

"(5) the Federal Aviation Act of 1958, by the Civil Aeronautics Board with respect to any air carrier or foreign air carrier subject to that Act; and

"(6) the Packers and Stockyards Act, 1921 (except as provided in section 406 of that Act), by the Secretary of Agriculture with respect to any activities subject to that Act.

"(c) For the purpose of the exercise by any agency referred to in subsection (b) of its powers under any Act referred to in that subsection, a violation of any requirement imposed under this title shall be deemed to be a violation of a requirement imposed under that Act. In addition to its powers under any provision of law specifically referred to in that subsection may exercise, for the purpose of enforcing compliance with any requirement imposed under this title any other authority conferred on it by law.

"Sec. 622. Relation to State laws

"This title does not annul, alter, affect, or exempt any person subject to the provisions of this title from complying with the laws of any State with respect to the collection, distribution, or use of any information on consumers, except to the extent that those laws are inconsistent with any provision of this title, and then only to the extent of the inconsistency."

EFFECTIVE DATE

Sec. 602. Section 504 of the Consumer Credit Protection Act is amended by adding at the end thereof the following new subsection:

"(d) Title VI takes effect upon the expiration of one hundred and eighty days following the date of its enactment."

And the Senate agree to the same.

Appendix IV

FAIR DEBT COLLECTION PRACTICES (FDCP)

You'll appreciate the FDCP if there's a collection agency harassing you. It is quite specific about what kind of collection tactics are illegal.

SUBCHAPTER V—DEBT COLLECTION PRACTICES

§ 1692. Congressional findings and declaration of purpose

(a) There is abundant evidence of the use of abusive, deceptive, and unfair debt collection practices by many debt collectors. Abusive debt collection practices contribute to the number of personal bankruptcies, to marital instability, to the loss of jobs, and to invasions of individual privacy.

(b) Existing laws and procedures for redressing these injuries are inadequate to protect consumers.

(c) Means other than misrepresentation or other abusive debt collection practices are available for the effective collection of debts.

(d) Abusive debt collection practices are carried on to a substantial extent in interstate commerce and through means and instrumentalities of such commerce. Even where abusive debt collection practices are purely intrastate in character, they nevertheless directly affect interstate commerce.

(e) It is the purpose of this subchapter to eliminate abusive debt collection practices by debt collectors, to insure that those debt collectors who refrain from using abusive debt collection practices are not competitively disadvantaged, and to promote consistent State action to protect consumers against debt collection abuses.

(Pub.L. 90–321, Title VIII, § 802, as added Pub.L. 95–109, Sept. 20, 1977, 91 Stat. 874.)

§ 1692a. Definitions

As used in this subchapter—

(1) The term "Commission" means the Federal Trade Commission.

(2) The term "communication" means the conveying of information regarding a debt directly or indirectly to any person through any medium.

(3) The term "consumer" means any natural person obligated or allegedly obligated to pay any debt.

(4) The term "creditor" means any person who offers or extends credit creating a debt or to whom a debt is owed, but such term does not include any person to the extent that he receives an assignment or transfer of a debt in default solely for the purpose of facilitating collection of such debt for another.

(5) The term "debt" means any obligation or alleged obligation of a consumer to pay money arising out of a transaction in which the money, property, insurance, or services which are the subject of the transaction are primarily for personal, family, or household purposes, whether or not such obligation has been reduced to judgment.

(6) The term "debt collector" means any person who uses any instrumentality of interstate commerce or the mails in any business the principal purpose of which is the collection of any debts, or who regularly collects or attempts to collect, directly or indirectly, debts owed or due or asserted to be owed or due another. Notwithstanding the exclusion provided by clause (G) of the last sentence of this para-

graph, the term includes any creditor who, in the process of collecting his own debts, uses any name other than his own which would indicate that a third person is collecting or attempting to collect such debts. For the purpose of section 1692f(6) of this title, such term also includes any person who uses any instrumentality of interstate commerce or the mails in any business the principal purpose of which is the enforcement of security interests. The term does not include—

(A) any officer or employee of a creditor while, in the name of the creditor, collecting debts for such creditor;

(B) any person while acting as a debt collector for another person, both of whom are related by common ownership or affiliated by corporate control, if the person acting as a debt collector does so only for persons to whom it is so related or affiliated and if the principal business of such person is not the collection of debts;

(C) any officer or employee of the United States or any State to the extent that collecting or attempting to collect any debt is in the performance of his official duties;

(D) any person while serving or attempting to serve legal process on any other person in connection with the judicial enforcement of any debt;

(E) any nonprofit organization which, at the request of consumers, performs bona fide consumer credit counseling and assists consumers in the liquidation of their debts by receiving payments from such consumers and distributing such amounts to creditor;

(F) any attorney-at-law collecting a debt as an attorney on behalf of and in the name of a client; and

(G) any person collecting or attempting to collect any debt owed or due or asserted to be owed or due another to the extent such activity (i) is incidental to a bona fide fiduciary obligation or a bona fide escrow arrangement; (ii) concerns a debt which was originated by such person; (iii) concerns a debt which was not in default at the time it was obtained by such person; or (iv) concerns a debt obtained by such person as a secured party in a commercial credit transaction involving the creditor.

(7) The term "location information" means a consumer's place of abode and his telephone number at such place, or his place of employment.

(8) The term "State" means any State, territory, or possession of the United States, the District of Columbia, the Commonwealth of Puerto Rico, or any political subdivision of any of the foregoing.

(Pub.L. 90–321, Title VIII, § 803, as added Pub.L. 95–109, Sept. 20, 1977, 91 Stat. 875.)

§ 1692b. Acquisition of location information

Any debt collector communicating with any person other than the consumer for the purpose of acquiring location information about the consumer shall—

(1) identify himself, state that he is confirming or correcting location information concerning the consumer, and, only if expressly requested, identify his employer;

(2) not state that such consumer owes any debt;

(3) not communicate with any such person more than once unless requested to do so by such person or unless the debt collector reasonably believes that the earlier response of such person is erroneous or incomplete and that such person now has correct or complete location information;

(4) not communicate by post card;

(5) not use any language or symbol on any envelope or in the contents of any communication effected by the mails or telegram that indicates that the debt collector is in the debt collection business or that the communication relates to the collection of a debt; and

(6) after the debt collector knows the consumer is represented by an attorney with regard to the subject debt and has knowledge of, or can readily ascertain, such attorney's name and address, not communicate with any person other than that attorney, unless the attorney fails to respond within a reasonable period of time to communication from the debt collector.

(Pub.L. 90–321, Title VIII, § 804, as added Pub.L. 95–109, Sept. 20, 1977, 91 Stat. 876.)

§ 1692c. Communication in connection with debt collection

(a) *Communication with the consumer generally*—Without the prior consent of the consumer given directly to the debt collector or the express permission of a court of competent jurisdiction, a debt collector may not communicate with a consumer in connection with the collection of any debt—

(1) at any unusual time or place or a time or place known or which should be known to be inconvenient to the consumer. In the absence of knowledge of circumstances to the contrary, a debt collector shall assume that the convenient time for communicating with a consumer is after 8 o'clock antemeridian and before 9 o'clock postmeridian, local time at the consumer's location;

(2) if the debt collector knows the consumer is represented by an attorney with respect to such debt and has knowledge of, or can readily ascertain, such attorney's name and address, unless the attorney fails to respond within a reasonable period of time to a communication

from the debt collector or unless the attorney consents to direct communication with the consumer; or

(3) at the consumer's place of employment if the debt collector knows or has reason to know that the consumer's employer prohibits the consumer from receiving such communication.

(b) *Communication with third parties*—Except as provided in section 1692b of this title, without the prior consent of the consumer given directly to the debt collector, or the express permission of a court of competent jurisdiction, or as reasonably necessary to effectuate a post-judgment judicial remedy, a debt collector may not communicate, in connection with the collection of any debt, with any person other than the consumer, his attorney, a consumer reporting agency if otherwise permitted by law, the creditor, the attorney of the creditor, or the attorney of the debt collector.

(c) *Ceasing communication*—If a consumer notifies a debt collector in writing that the consumer refuses to pay a debt or that the consumer wishes the debt collector to cease further communication with the consumer, the debt collector shall not communicate further with the consumer with respect to such debt, except—

(1) to advise the consumer that the debt collector's further efforts are being terminated;

(2) to notify the consumer that the debt collector or creditor may invoke specified remedies which are ordinarily invoked by such debt collector or creditor; or

(3) where applicable, to notify the consumer that the debt collector or creditor intends to invoke a specified remedy.

If such notice from the consumer is made by mail, notification shall be complete upon receipt.

(d) *Definitions*—For the purpose of this section, the term "consumer" includes the consumer's spouse, parent (if the consumer is a minor), guardian, executor, or administrator.

(Pub.L. 90–321, Title VIII, § 805, as added Pub.L. 95–109, Sept. 20, 1977, 91 Stat. 876.)

§ 1692d. Harassment or abuse

A debt collector may not engage in any conduct the natural consequence of which is to harass, oppress, or abuse any person in connection with the collection of a debt. Without limiting the general application of the foregoing, the following conduct is a violation of this section:

(1) The use or threat of use of violence or other criminal means to harm the physical person, reputation, or property of any person.

(2) The use of obscene or profane language or language the natural consequence of which is to abuse the hearer or reader.

(3) The publication of a list of consumers who allegedly refuse to pay debts, except to a consumer reporting agency or to persons meeting the requirements of section 1681a(f) or 1681b(3) of this title.

(4) The advertisement for sale of any debt to coerce payment of the debt.

(5) Causing a telephone to ring or engaging any person in telephone conversation repeatedly or continuously with intent to annoy, abuse, or harass any person at the called number.

(6) Except as provided in section 1692b of this title, the placement of telephone calls without meaningful disclosure of the caller's identity.

(Pub.L. 90–321, Title VIII, § 806, as added Pub.L. 95–109, Sept. 20, 1977, 91 Stat. 877.)

§ 1692e. False or misleading representations

A debt collector may not use any false, deceptive, or misleading representation or means in connection with the collection of any debt. Without limiting the general application of the foregoing, the following conduct is a violation of this section:

(1) The false representation or implication that the debt collector is vouched for, bonded by, or affiliated with the United States or any State, including the use of any badge, uniform, or facsimile thereof.

(2) The false representation of—

(A) the character, amount, or legal status of any debt; or

(B) any services rendered or compensation which may be lawfully received by any debt collector for the collection of a debt.

(3) The false representation or implication that any individual is an attorney or that any communication is from an attorney.

(4) The representation or implication that nonpayment of any debt will result in the arrest or imprisonment of any person or the seizure, garnishment, attachment, or sale of any property or wages of any person unless such action is lawful and the debt collector or creditor intends to take such action.

(5) The threat to take any action that cannot legally be taken or that is not intended to be taken.

(6) The false representation or implication that a sale, referral, or other transfer of any interest in a debt shall cause the consumer to—

(A) lose any claim or defense to payment of the debt; or

(B) become subject to any practice prohibited by this subchapter.

(7) The false representation or implication that the consumer committed any crime or other conduct in order to disgrace the consumer.

(8) Communicating or threatening to communicate to any person credit information which is known or which should be known to be false, including the failure to communicate that a disputed debt is disputed.

(9) The use or distribution of any written communication which simulates or is falsely represented to be a document authorized, issued, or approved by any court, official, or agency of the United States or any State, or which creates a false impression as to its source, authorization, or approval.

(10) The use of any false representation or deceptive means to collect or attempt to collect any debt or to obtain information concerning a consumer.

(11) Except as otherwise provided for communications to acquire location information under section 1692b of this title, the failure to disclose clearly in all communications made to collect a debt or to obtain information about a consumer, that the debt collector is attempting to collect a debt and that any information obtained will be used for that purpose.

(12) The false representation or implication that accounts have been turned over to innocent purchasers for value.

(13) The false representation or implication that documents are legal process.

(14) The use of any business, company, or organization name other than the true name of the debt collector's business, company, or organization.

(15) The false representation or implication that documents are not legal process forms or do not require action by the consumer.

(16) The false representation or implication that a debt collector operates or is employed by a consumer reporting agency as defined by section 1681a(f) of this title.

(Pub.L. 90–321, Title VIII, § 807, as added Pub.L. 95–109, Sept. 20, 1977, 91 Stat. 877.)

§ 1692f. Unfair practices

A debt collector may not use unfair or unconscionable means to collect or attempt to collect any debt. Without limiting the general application of the foregoing, the following conduct is a violation of this section:

(1) The collection of any amount (including any interest, fee, charge, or expense incidental to the principal obligation) unless such amount is expressly authorized by the agreement creating the debt or permitted by law.

(2) The acceptance by a debt collector from any person of a check or other payment instrument postdated by more than five days unless such person is notified in writing of the debt collector's intent to deposit such check or instrument not more than ten nor less than three business days prior to such deposit.

(3) The solicitation by a debt collector of any postdated check or other postdated payment instrument for the purpose of threatening or instituting criminal prosecution.

(4) Depositing or threatening to deposit any postdated check or other postdated payment instrument prior to the date on such check or instrument.

(5) Causing charges to be made to any person for communications by concealment of the true purpose of the communication. Such charges include, but are not limited to, collect telephone calls and telegram fees.

(6) Taking or threatening to take any nonjudicial action to effect dispossession or disablement of property if—

(A) there is no present right to possession of the property claimed as collateral through an enforceable security interest;

(B) there is no present intention to take possession of the property; or

(C) the property is exempt by law from such dispossession or disablement.

(7) Communicating with a consumer regarding a debt by post card.

(8) Using any language or symbol, other than the debt collector's address, on any envelope when communicating with a consumer by use of the mails or by telegram, except that a debt collector may use his business name if such name does not indicate that he is in the debt collection business.

(Pub.L. 90–321, Title VIII, § 808, as added Pub.L. 95–109, Sept. 20, 1977, 91 Stat. 879.)

§ 1692g. Validation of debts

Notice of debt; contents

(a) Within five days after the initial communication with a consumer in connection with the collection of any debt, a debt collector shall, unless the following information is contained in the initial communication or the consumer has paid the debt, send the consumer a written notice containing—

(1) the amount of the debt;

(2) the name of the creditor to whom the debt is owed;

(3) a statement that unless the consumer, within thirty days after receipt of the notice, disputes the validity of the debt, or any

portion thereof, the debt will be assumed to be valid by the debt collector;

(4) a statement that if the consumer notifies the debt collector in writing within the thirty-day period that the debt, or any portion thereof, is disputed, the debt collector will obtain verification of the debt or a copy of a judgment against the consumer and a copy of such verification or judgment will be mailed to the consumer by the debt collector; and

(5) a statement that, upon the consumer's written request within the thirty-day period, the debt collector will provide the consumer with the name and address of the original creditor, if different from the current creditor.

Disputed debts

(b) If the consumer notifies the debt collector in writing within the thirty-day period described in subsection (a) of this section that the debt, or any portion thereof, is disputed, or that the consumer requests the name and address of the original creditor, the debt collector shall cease collection of the debt, or any disputed portion thereof, until the debt collector obtains verification of the debt or a copy of a judgment, or the name and address of the original creditor, and a copy of such verification or judgment, or name and address of the original creditor, is mailed to the consumer by the debt collector.

Admission of liability

(c) The failure of a consumer to dispute the validity of a debt under this section may not be construed by any court as an admission of liability by the consumer.

(Pub.L. 90–321, Title VIII, § 809, as added Pub.L. 95–109, Sept. 20, 1977, 91 Stat. 879.)

§ 1692h. Multiple debts

If any consumer owes multiple debts and makes any single payment to any debt collector with respect to such debts, such debt collector may not apply such payment to any debt which is disputed by the consumer and, where applicable, shall apply such payment in accordance with the consumer's directions.

(Pub.L. 90–321, Title VIII, § 810, as added Pub.L. 95–109, Sept. 20, 1977, 91 Stat. 880.)

§ 1692i. Legal actions by debt collectors

(a) Any debt collector who brings any legal action on a debt against any consumer shall—

(1) in the case of an action to enforce an interest in real property securing the consumer's obligation, bring such action only in a judicial

district or similar legal entity in which such real property is located; or

    (2) in the case of an action not described in paragraph (1), bring such action only in the judicial district or similar legal entity—

        (A) in which such consumer signed the contract sued upon; or

        (B) in which such consumer resides at the commencement of the action.

    (b) Nothing in this subchapter shall be construed to authorize the bringing of legal actions by debt collectors.

    (Pub.L. 90–321, Title VIII, § 811, as added Pub.L. 95–109, Sept. 20, 1977, 91 Stat. 880.)

§ 1692j. Furnishing certain deceptive forms

    (a) It is unlawful to design, compile, and furnish any form knowing that such form would be used to create the false belief in a consumer that a person other than the creditor of such consumer is participating in the collection of or in an attempt to collect a debt such consumer allegedly owes such creditor, when in fact such person is not so participating.

    (b) Any person who violates this section shall be liable to the same extent and in the same manner as a debt collector is liable under section 1692k of this title for failure to comply with a provision of this subchapter.

    (Pub.L. 90–321, Title VIII, § 812, as added Pub.L. 95–109, Sept. 20, 1977, 91 Stat. 880.)

§ 1692k. Civil liability

Amount of damages

    (a) Except as otherwise provided by this section, any debt collector who fails to comply with any provision of this subchapter with respect to any person is liable to such person in an amount equal to the sum of—

        (1) any actual damage sustained by such person as a result of such failure;

        (2)(A) in the case of any action by an individual, such additional damages as the court may allow, but not exceeding $1,000; or

        (B) in the case of a class action, (i) such amount for each named plaintiff as could be recovered under subparagraph (A), and (ii) such amount as the court may allow for all other class members, without regard to a minimum individual recovery, not to exceed the lesser of $500,000 or 1 per centum of the net worth of the debt collector; and

        (3) in the case of any successful action to enforce the foregoing liability, the costs of the action, together with a reasonable attorney's fee as determined by the court. On a finding by the court that an

action under this section was brought in bad faith and for the purpose of harassment, the court may award to the defendant attorney's fees reasonable in relation to the work expended and costs.

Factors considered by court

(b) In determining the amount of liability in any action under subsection (a) of this section, the court shall consider, among other relevant factors—

(1) in any individual action under subsection (a)(2)(A) of this section, the frequency and persistence of noncompliance by the debt collector, the nature of such noncompliance, and the extent to which such noncompliance was intentional; or

(2) in any class action under subsection (a)(2)(B) of this section, the frequency and persistence of noncompliance by the debt collector, the nature of such noncompliance, the resources of the debt collector, the number of persons adversely affected, and the extent to which the debt collector's noncompliance was intentional.

Intent

(c) A debt collector may not be held liable in any action brought under this subchapter if the debt collector shows by a preponderance of evidence that the violation was not intentional and resulted from a bona fide error notwithstanding the maintenance of procedures reasonably adapted to avoid any such error.

Jurisdiction

(d) An action to enforce any liability created by this subchapter may be brought in any appropriate United States district court without regard to the amount in controversy, or in any other court of competent jurisdiction, within one year from the date on which the violation occurs.

Advisory opinions of Commission

(e) No provision of this section imposing any liability shall apply to any act done or omitted in good faith in conformity with any advisory opinion of the Commission, notwithstanding that after such act or omission has occurred, such opinion is amended, rescinded, or determined by judicial or other authority to be invalid for any reason.

(Pub.L. 90–321, Title VIII, § 813, as added Pub.L. 95–109, Sept. 20, 1977, 91 Stat. 881.)

Appendix V

FAIR CREDIT BILLING ACT (FCBA)

The FCBA is key to many of the dispute tactics in this book, because it puts a burden on many creditors to bill you in a certain manner before a debt can be considered late. In many situations, it protects you from being considered late in payment if you contest part of a bill.

TITLE III—FAIR CREDIT BILLING

"Sec. 301. Short title

This title may be cited as the "Fair Credit Billing Act."

"Sec. 302. Declaration of purpose

The last sentence of section 102 of the Truth in Lending Act (15 U.S.C. 1601) is amended by striking out the period and inserting in lieu thereof a comma and the following: "and to protect the consumer against inaccurate and unfair credit billing and credit card practices."

"Sec. 303. Definitions of creditor and open end credit plan

The first sentence of section 103 (f) of the Truth in Lending Act (15 U.S.C. 1602 (f)) is amended to read as follows: "The term 'creditor' refers only to creditors who regularly extend, or arrange for the extension of, credit which is payable by agreement in more than four installments or for which the payment of a finance charge is or may be required, whether in connection with loans, sales of property or services, or otherwise. For the purposes of the requirements imposed under Chapter 4 and sections 127 (a)(6), 127 (a)(7), 127 (a)(8), 127 (b)(1), 127 (b)(2), 127 (b)(3), 127 (b)(9), and 127 (b)(11) of Chapter 2 of this Title, the term 'creditor' shall also include card issuers whether or not the amount due is payable by agreement in more than four installments or the payment of a finance charge is or may be required, and the Board shall, by regulation, apply these requirements to such card issuers, to the extent appropriate, even though the requirements are by their terms applicable only to creditors offering open end credit plans.

"Sec. 304. Disclosure of fair credit billing rights

"(a) Section 127 (a) of the Truth in Lending Act (15 U.S.C. 1637 (a)) is amended by adding at the end thereof a new paragraph as follows:

"(8) A statement, in a form prescribed by regulations of the Board of the protection provided by sections 161 and 170 to an obligor and the creditor's responsibilities under sections 162 and 170. With respect to each of two billing cycles per year, at semiannual intervals, the creditor shall transmit such statement to each obligor to whom the creditor is required to transmit a statement pursuant to section 127 (b) for such billing cycle."

"(b) Section 127 (c) of such Act (15 U.S.C. 1637 (c)) is amended to read:

"(c) In the case of any existing account under an open end consumer credit plan having an outstanding balance of more than $1 at or after the close of the creditor's first full billing cycle under the plan after the effective date of subsection (a) or any amendments thereto, the items described in subsection (a), to the extent applicable and not previously disclosed, shall be disclosed in a notice mailed or delivered to the obligor not later than the time of mailing the next statement required by subsection (b)."

"Sec. 305. Disclosure of billing contact

Section 127 (b) of the Truth in Lending Act (15 U.S.C. 1637 (b)) is amended by adding at the end thereof a new paragraph as follows:

"(11) The address to be used by the creditor for the purpose of receiving billing inquiries from the obligor."

"Sec. 306. Billing practices

The Truth in Lending Act (15 U.S.C. 1601-1665) is amended by adding at the end thereof a new chapter as follows:

"Chapter 4—Credit Billing'

"Sec. 161. Correction of billing errors:

"(a) If a creditor, within sixty days after having transmitted to an obligor a statement of the obligor's account in connection with an extension of consumer credit, receives at the address disclosed under section 127 (b)(11) a written notice (other than notice on a payment stub or other payment medium supplied by the creditor if the creditor so stipulates with the disclosure required under section 127 (a)(8)) from the obligor in which the obligor—

"(1) sets forth or otherwise enables the creditor to identify the name and account number (if any) of the obligor,

"(2) indicates the obligor's belief that the statement contains a billing error and the amount of such billing error, and

"(3) sets forth the reasons for the obligor's belief (to the extent applicable) that the statement contains a billing error, the creditor shall, unless the obligor has, after giving such written notice and before the expiration of the time limits herein specified, agreed that the statement was correct—

"(A) not later than thirty days after the receipt of the notice, send a written acknowledgement thereof to the obligor, unless the action required in subparagraph (B) is taken within such thirty-day period, and

"(B) not later than two complete billing cycles of the creditor (in no event later than ninety days) after the receipt of the notice and prior to taking any action to collect the amount, or any part thereof, indicated by the obligor under paragraph (2) either—

"(i) make appropriate corrections in the account of this obligor, including the crediting of any finance charges on amounts erroneously billed, and transmit to the obligor a notification of such corrections and the creditor's explanation of any change in the amount indicated by the obligor under paragraph (2) and, if any such change is made and the obligor so requests, copies of documentary evidence of the obligor's indebtedness; or

"(ii) send a written explanation or clarification to the obligor, after having conducted an investigation, setting forth to the extent applicable the reasons why the creditor believes the account of the obligor was correctly shown in the statement and, upon request of the obligor, provide copies of documentary evidence of the obligor's indebtedness. In the case of a billing error where the obligor alleges that the creditor's billing statement reflects goods not delivered to the obligor or his designee in accordance with the agreement made at the time of the transaction, a creditor may not construe such amount to be correctly shown unless he determines that such goods were actually delivered, mailed, or otherwise sent to the obligor and provides the obligor with a statement of such determination.

After complying with the provisions of this subsection with respect to an alleged billing error, a creditor has no further responsibility under this section if the obligor continues to make substantially the same allegation with respect to such error.

"(b) For the purpose of this section, a 'billing error' consists of any of the following:

"(1) A reflection on a statement of an extension of credit which was not made to the obligor or, if made, was not in the amount reflected on such statement.

"(2) A reflection on a statement of an extension of credit for which the obligor requests additional clarification including documentary evidence thereof.

"(3) A reflection on a statement of goods or services not accepted by the obligor or his designee or not delivered to the obligor or his designee in accordance with the agreement made at the time of a transaction.

"(4) The creditor's failure to reflect properly on a statement a payment made by the obligor or a credit issued to the obligor.

"(5) A computation error or similar error of an accounting nature of the creditor on a statement.

"(6) Any other error described in regulations of the Board.

"(c) For the purposes of this section, 'action to collect the amount', or any part thereof, indicated by an obligor under paragraph (2) does not include the sending of statements of account to the obligor following written notice from the obligor as specified under subsection (a), if—

"(1) the obligor's account is not restricted or closed because of the failure of the obligor to pay the amount indicated under paragraph (2) of subsection (a), and

"(2) the creditor indicates the payment of such amount is not required pending the creditor's compliance with this section.

Nothing in this section shall be construed to prohibit any action by a creditor to collect any amount which has not been indicated by the obligor to contain a billing error.

"(d) Pursuant to regulations of the Board, a creditor operating an open end consumer credit plan may not, prior to the sending of the written explanation or clarification required under paragraph (B) (ii), restrict or close an account with respect to which the obligor has indicated pursuant to subsection (a) that he believes such account to contain a billing error solely because of the obligor's failure to pay the amount indicated to be in error. Nothing in this subsection shall be deemed to prohibit a creditor from applying against the credit limit on the obligor's account the amount indicated to be in error.

"(e) Any creditor who fails to comply with the requirements of this section or section 162 forfeits any right to collect from the obligor the amount indicated by the obligor under paragraph (2) of subsection (a) of this section, and any finance charges thereon, except that the amount required to be forfeited under this subsection may not exceed $50.

"Sec. 162. Regulation of credit reports

"(a) After receiving a notice from an obligor as provided in section 161 (a), a creditor or his agent may not directly or indirectly threaten to report to any person adversely on the obligor's credit rating or credit standing because of the obligor's failure to pay the amount indicated by the obligor under section 161 (a)(2), and such amount may not be reported as delinquent to any third party until the creditor has met the requirements of section 161 and has allowed the obligor the same number of days (not less than ten) thereafter to make payment as is provided under the credit agreement with the obligor for the payment of undisputed amounts.

"(b) If a creditor receives a further written notice from an obligor that an amount is still in dispute within the time allowed for payment under subsection (a) of this section, a creditor may not report to any third party that the amount of the obligor is delinquent because the obligor has failed to pay an amount which he has indicated under section 161 (a)(2), unless the creditor also reports that the amount is in dispute and, at the same time, notifies the obligor of the name and address of each party to whom the creditor is reporting information concerning the delinquency.

"(c) A creditor shall report any subsequent resolution of any delinquencies reported pursuant to subsection (b) to the parties to whom such delinquencies were initially reported.

"Sec. 163. Length of billing period

"(a) If an open end consumer credit plan provides a time period within which an obligor may repay any portion of the credit extended without incurring an additional finance charge, such additional finance charge may not be imposed with respect to such portion of the credit extended for the billing cycle of which such period is a part unless a statement which includes the amount upon which the finance charge for that period is based was mailed at least fourteen days prior to the date specified in the statement by which payment must be made in order to avoid imposition of that finance charge.

"(b) Subsection (a) does not apply in any case where a creditor has been prevented, delayed, or hindered in making timely mailing or delivery of such periodic statement within the time period specified in such subsection because of an act of God, war, natural disaster, strike, or other excusable or justifiable cause, as determined under regulations of the Board.

"Sec. 164. Prompt crediting of payments

"Payments received from an obligor under an open end consumer credit plan by the creditor shall be posted promptly to the obligor's account as specified in regulations of the Board. Such regulations shall prevent a finance charge from being imposed on any obligor if the creditor has received the obligor's payment in readily identifiable form in the amount, manner, location, and time indicated by the credit to avoid the imposition thereof.

"Sec. 165. Crediting excess payments

"Whenever an obligor transmits funds to a creditor in excess of the total balance due on an open end consumer credit account, the creditor shall promptly (1) upon request of the obligor refund the amount of the overpayment, or (2) credit such amount to the obligor's account.

"Sec. 166. Prompt notification of returns

"With respect to any sales transaction where a credit card has been used to obtain credit, where the seller is a person other than the card issuer, and where the seller accepts or allows a return of the goods or forgiveness of a debit for services which were the subject of such sale, the seller shall promptly transmit to the credit card issuer, a credit statement with respect thereto and the credit card issuer shall credit the account of the obligor for the amount of the transaction.

"Sec. 167. Use of cash discounts

"(a) With respect to credit card which may be used for extensions of credit in sales transactions in which the seller is a person other than the card issuer; the card issuer may not, by contract or otherwise, prohibit any such seller from offering a discount to a cardholder to induce the cardholder to pay by cash, check, or similar means rather than use a credit card.

"(b) With respect to any sales transaction, and discount not in excess of 5 per centum offered by the seller for the purpose of inducing payment by cash, check, or other means not involving the use of a credit card shall not constitute a finance charge as determined under section 106, if such discount is offered to all prospective buyers and its availability is disclosed to all prospective buyers clearly and conspicuously in accordance with regulations of the Board.

"Sec. 168. Prohibition of tie-in services

"Notwithstanding any agreement to the contrary, a card issuer may not require a seller, as a condition to participating in a credit card plan, to open an account with or procure any other service from the card issuer or its subsidiary or agent.

"Sec. 169. Prohibition of offsets

"(a) A card issuer may not take any action to offset a cardholder's indebtedness arising in connection with a consumer credit transaction under the relevant credit card plan against funds of the cardholder held on deposit with the card issuer unless—

"(1) such action was previously authorized in writing by the cardholder in accordance with a credit plan whereby the cardholder agrees periodically to pay debts incurred in his open end credit account by permitting the card issuer periodically to deduct all or a portion of such debt from the cardholder's deposit account, and

"(2) such action with respect to any outstanding disputed amount not be taken by the card issuer upon request of the cardholder. In the case of any credit card account in existence on the effective date of this section, the previous written authorization referred to in clause (1) shall not be required until the date (after such effective date) when such account is renewed, but in no case later than one year after such effective date. Such written authorization shall be deemed to exist if the card issuer has previously notified the cardholder that the use of his credit card account will subject any funds which the card issuer holds in deposit accounts of such cardholder to offset against any amounts due and payable on his credit card account which have not been paid in accordance with the terms of the agreement between the card issuer and the cardholder.

"(b) This section does not alter or affect the right under State law of a card issuer to attach or otherwise levy upon funds of a cardholder held on deposit with the card issuer if that remedy is constitutionally available to creditors generally.

"Sec. 170. Rights of credit card customers

"(a) Subject to the limitation contained in subsection (b), a card issuer who has issued a credit card to a cardholder pursuant to an open end consumer credit plan shall be subject to all claims (other than tort claims) and defenses arising out of any transaction in which the credit card is used as a method of payment or extension of credit if (1) the obligor has made a good faith attempt to obtain satisfactory resolution of a disagreement or problem relative to the transaction from the person honoring the credit card; (2) the amount of the initial transaction exceeds $50; and (3) the place where the initial transaction occurred was in the same State as the mailing address previously provided by the cardholder or was within 100 miles from such address, except that the limitations set forth in clauses (2) and (3) with respect to an obligor's right to asset claims and defenses against a card issuer shall not be applicable to any transaction in which the person honoring the credit card (A) is the same person as the card issuer, (B) is controlled by the card issuer, (C) is under direct or indirect common control with the card issuer, (D) is a franchised dealer in the card issuer's products or services, or (E) has obtained the order for such transaction through a mail solicitation made by or participated in by the card issuer in which the cardholder is solicited to enter into such transaction by using the credit card issued by the card issuer.

"(b) The amount of claims or defenses asserted by the cardholder may not exceed the amount of credit outstanding with respect to such transaction at the time the cardholder first notifies the card issuer or the person honoring the credit card of such claim or defense. For the purpose of determining the amount of credit outstanding in the preceding sentence, payments and credits to the cardholder's account are deemed to have been applied, in the order indicated, to the payment of: (1) late charges in the order of their entry to the account; (2) finance charges in order of their entry to the account; and (3) debits to the account other than those set forth above, in the order in which each debit entry to the account was made.

"Sec. 171. Relation to State laws

"(a) This chapter does not annul, alter, or affect, or exempt any person subject to the provisions of this chapter from complying with, the laws of any State with respect to credit billing practices, except to the extent that those laws are inconsistent with any provision of this chapter, and then only to the extent of the inconsistency. The Board may not determine that any State law is inconsistent with any provision of this chapter if the Board determines that such law gives greater protection to the consumer.

"(b) The Board shall by regulation exempt from the requirements of this chapter any class of credit transactions within any State if it determines that under the law of that State that class of transactions is subject to requirements substantially similar to those imposed under this chapter or that such law gives greater protection to the consumer, and that there is adequate provision for enforcement."

Appendix VI

TRUTH IN LENDING ACT (TLA)

The TLA helps spell out consumer rights in mortgages and leases. Truth in Lending focuses on issues such as finance charges, fees, and surcharges to credit transactions, as well as mandatory disclosures and consumers rights to break contracts within 3 days of signing. The act also covers the issue of payment deadlines and can therefore be useful in making an argument about the relative lateness of payment with regard to a loan agreement.

CONSUMER CREDIT PROTECTION ACT

Public Law 90-321; 82 Stat. 146

An Act to safeguard the consumer in connection with the utilization of credit by requiring full disclosure of the terms and conditions of finance charges in credit transactions or in offers to extend credit; by restricting the garnishment of wages; and by creating the National Commission on Consumer Finance to study and make recommendations on the need for further regulation of the consumer finance industry; and for other purposes.

Be it enacted by the Senate and House of Representatives of the United States of America in Congress assembled, That:

"Sec. 1. Short title of entire Act

This Act may be cited as the Consumer Credit Protection Act.

TITLE I—CONSUMER CREDIT COST DISCLOSURE

Chapter
1. GENERAL PROVISIONS   101
2. CREDIT TRANSACTIONS   121
3. CREDIT ADVERTISING   141

Chapter 1—General Provisions

"Sec. 101. Short title

This title may be cited as the Truth in Lending Act.

"Sec. 102. Findings and declaration of purpose

The Congress finds that economic stabilization would be enhanced and the competition among the various financial institutions and other firms engaged in the extension of consumer credit would be strengthened by the informed use of credit. The informed use of credit results from an awareness of the cost thereof by consumers. It is the purpose of this title to assure a meaningful disclosure of credit terms so that the consumer will be able to compare more readily the various credit terms available to him and avoid the uninformed use of credit.

"Sec. 103. Definitions and rules of construction

"(a) The definitions and rules of construction set forth in this section are applicable for the purposes of this title.

"(b) The term 'Board' refers to the Board of Governors of the Federal Reserve System.

"(c) The term 'organization' means a corporation, government or governmental subdivision or agency, trust, estate, partnership, cooperative, or association.

"(d) The term 'person' means a natural person or an organization.

"(e) The term 'credit' means the right granted by a creditor to a debtor to defer payment of debt or to incur debt and defer its payment.

"(f) The term 'creditor' refers only to creditors who regularly extend, or arrange for the extension of, credit for which the payment of a finance charge is required, whether in connection with loans, sales of property or services, or otherwise. The provisions of this title apply to any such creditor, irrespective of his or its status as a natural person or any type of organization.

"(g) The term 'credit sale' refers to any sale with respect to which credit is extended or arranged by the seller. The term includes any contract in the form of a bailment or lease if the bailee or lessee contracts to pay as compensation for use a sum substantially equivalent to or in excess of the aggregate value of the property and services involved and it is agreed that the bailee or lessee will become, or for no other or a nominal consideration has the option to become, the owner of the property upon full compliance with his obligations under the contract.

"(h) The adjective 'consumer', used with reference to a credit transaction, characterizes the transaction as one in which the party to whom credit is offered or extended is a natural person, and the money, property, or services which are the subject of the transaction are primarily for personal, family, household, or agricultural purposes.

"(i) The term 'open end credit plan' refers to a plan prescribing the terms of credit transactions which may be made thereunder from time to time and under the terms of which a finance charge may be computed on the outstanding unpaid balance from time to time thereunder.

"(j) The term 'State' refers to any State, the Commonwealth of Puerto Rico, the District of Columbia, and any territory or possession of the United States.

"(k) Any reference to any requirement imposed under this title or any provision thereof includes reference to the regulations of the Board under this title or the provision thereof in question.

"(l) The disclosure of an amount or percentage which is greater than the amount or percentage required to be disclosed under this title does not in itself constitute a violation of this title.

"Sec. 104. Exempted transactions

This title does not apply to the following:

"(1) Credit transactions involving extensions of credit for business or commercial purposes, or to government or governmental agencies or instrumentalities, or to organizations.

"(2) Transactions in securities or commodities accounts by a broker-dealer registered with the Securities and Exchange Commission.

"(3) Credit transactions, other than real property transactions, in which the total amount to be financed exceeds $25,000.

"(4) Transactions under public utility tariffs, if the Board determines that a State regulatory body regulates the charges for the public utility services involved, the charges for delayed payment, and any discount allowed for early payment.

"Sec. 105. Regulations

The Board shall prescribe regulations to carry out the purposes of this title. These regulations may contain such classifications, differentiations, or other provisions, and may provide for such adjustments and exceptions for any class of transactions, as in the judgment of the Board are necessary or proper to effectuate the purposes of this title, to prevent circumvention or evasion thereof, or to facilitate compliance therewith.

"Sec. 106. Determination of finance charge

"(a) Except as otherwise provided in this section, the amount of the finance charge in connection with any consumer credit transaction shall be determined as the sum of all charges, payable directly or indirectly by the person to whom the credit is extended, and imposed directly or indirectly by the creditor as an incident to the extension of credit, including any of the following types of charges which are applicable:

"(1) Interest, time price differential, and any amount payable under a point, discount, or other system of additional charges.

"(2) Service or carrying charge.

"(3) Loan fee, finder's fee, or similar charge.

"(4) Fee for an investigation or credit report.

"(5) Premium or other charge for any guarantee or insurance protecting the creditor against the obligor's default or other credit loss.

"(b) Charges or premiums for credit life, accident, or health insurance written in connection with any consumer credit transaction shall be included in the finance charge unless

"(1) the coverage of the debtor by the insurance is not a factor in the approval by the creditor of the extension of credit, and this fact is clearly disclosed in writing to the person applying for or obtaining the extension of credit; and

"(2) in order to obtain the insurance in connection with the extension of credit, the person to whom the credit is extended must give specific affirmative written indication of his desire to do so after written disclosure to him of the cost thereof.

"(c) Charges or premiums for insurance, written in connection with any consumer credit transaction, against loss of or damage to property or against liability arising out of the ownership or use of property, shall be included in the finance charge unless a clear and specific statement in writing is furnished by the creditor to the person to whom the credit is extended, setting forth the cost of the insurance if obtained from or through the creditor, and stating that the person to whom the credit is extended may choose the person through which the insurance is to be obtained.

"(d) If any of the following items is itemized and disclosed in accordance with the regulations of the Board in connection with any transaction, then the creditor need not include that item in the computation of the finance charge with respect to that transaction:

"(1) Fees and charges prescribed by law which actually are or will be paid to public officials for determining the existence of or for perfecting or releasing or satisfying any security related to the credit transaction.

"(2) The premium payable for an insurance in lieu of perfecting any security interest otherwise required by the creditor in connection with the transaction, if the premium does not exceed the fees and charges described in paragraph (1) which would otherwise be payable.

"(3) Taxes.

"(4) Any other type of charge which is not for credit and the exclusion of which from the finance charge is approved by the Board by regulation.

"(e) The following items, when charged in connection with any extension of credit secured by an interest in real property, shall not be included in the computation of the finance charge with respect to that transaction:

"(1) Fees or premiums for title examination, title insurance, or similar purposes.

"(2) Fees for preparation of a deed, settlement statement, or other documents.

"(3) Escrows for future payments of taxes and insurance.

"(4) Fees for notarizing deeds and other documents.

"(5) Appraisal fees.

"(6) Credit reports.

"Sec. 107. Determination of annual percentage rate

"(a) The annual percentage rate applicable to any extension of consumer credit shall be determined, in accordance with the regulations of the Board,

"(1) in the case of any extension of credit other than under an open end credit plan, as

"(A) that nominal annual percentage rate which will yield a sum equal to the amount of the finance charge when it is applied to the unpaid balances of the amount financed, calculated according to the actuarial method of allocating payments made on a debt between the amount financed and the amount of the finance charge, pursuant to which a payment is applied first to the accumulated finance charge and the balance is applied to the unpaid amount financed; or

"(B) the rate determined by any method prescribed by the Board as a method which materially simplifies computation while retaining reasonable accuracy as compared with the rate determined under subparagraph (A).

"(2) in the case of any extension of credit under an open end credit plan, as the quotient (expressed as a percentage) of the total finance charge for the period to which it relates divided by the amount upon which the finance charge for that period is based, multiplied by the number of such periods in a year.

"(b) Where a creditor imposes the same finance charge for balances within a specified range, the annual percentage rate shall be computed on the median balance within the range, except that if the Board determines that a rate so computed would not be meaningful, or would be materially misleading, the annual percentage rate shall be computed on such other basis as the Board may be regulation required.

"(c) The annual percentage rate may be rounded to the nearest quarter of 1 per centum for credit transactions payable in substantially equal installments when a creditor determines the total finance charge on the basis of a single add-on, discount, periodic, or other rate, and the rate is converted into an annual percentage rate under procedures prescribed by the Board.

"(d) The Board may authorize the use of rate tables or charts which may provide for the disclosure of annual percentage rates which vary from the rate determined in accordance with subsection (a) (1) (A) by not more than such tolerances as the Board may allow. The Board may not allow a tolerance greater than 8 per centum of that rate except to simplify compliance where irregular payments are involved.

"(e) In the case of creditors determining the annual percentage rate in a manner other than as described in subsection (c) or (d), the Board may authorize other reasonable tolerances.

"(f) Prior to January 1, 1971, any rate required under this title to be disclosed as a percentage rate may, at the option of the creditor, be expressed in the form of the corresponding ratio of dollars per hundred dollars.

"Sec. 108. Administrative enforcement

"(a) Compliance with the requirements imposed under this title shall be enforced under

"(1) section 8 of the Federal Deposit Insurance Act, in the case of

"(A) national banks, by the Comptroller of the Currency.

"(B) member banks of the Federal Reserve System (other than national banks), by the Board.

"(C) banks insured by the Federal Deposit Insurance Corporation (other than members of the Federal Reserve System), by the Board of Directors of the Federal Deposit Insurance Corporation.

"(2) section 5 (d) of the Home Owners' Loan Act of 1933, section 407 of the National Housing Act, and sections 6 (f) and 17 of the Federal Home Loan Bank Act, by the Federal Home Loan Bank Board (acting directly or through the Federal Savings and Loan Insurance Corporation), in the case of any institution subject to any of those provisions.

"(3) the Federal Credit Union Act, by the Director of the Bureau of Federal Credit Unions with respect to any Federal credit union.

"(4) the Acts to regulate commerce, by the Interstate Commerce Commission with respect to any common carrier subject to those Acts.

"(5) the Federal Aviation Act of 1958, by the Civil Aeronautics Board with respect to any air carrier or foreign air carrier subject to that Act.

"(6) the Packers and Stockyards Act, 1921 (except as provided in section 406 of that Act), by the Secretary of Agriculture with respect to any activities subject to that Act.

"(b) For the Purpose of the Exercise by any agency referred to in subsection (a) of its powers under any Act referred to in that subsection, a violation of any requirement imposed under this title shall be deemed to be a violation of any requirement imposed under this title shall be deemed to be a violation of a requirement imposed under that Act. In addition to its powers under any provision of law specifically referred to in subsection (a), each of the agencies referred to in that subsection may exercise, for the purpose of enforcing compliance with any requirement imposed under this title, any other authority conferred on it by law.

"(c) Except to the extent that enforcement of the requirements imposed under this title is specifically committed to some other Government agency under subsection (a), the Federal Trade Commission shall enforce such requirements. For the purpose of the exercise by the Federal

Trade Commission of its functions and powers under the Federal Trade Commission Act, a violation of any requirement imposed under that Act. All of the functions and powers of the Federal Trade Commission under the Federal Trade Commission Act are available to the Commission to enforce compliance by any person with the requirements imposed under this title, irrespective of whether that person is engaged in commerce or meets any other jurisdictional tests in the Federal Trade Commission Act.

"(d) The authority of the Board to issue regulations under this title does not impair the authority of any other agency designated in this section to make rules respecting its own procedures in enforcing compliance with requirements imposed under this title.

"Sec. 109. Views of other agencies

In the exercise of its functions under this title, the Board may obtain upon request the views of any other Federal agency which, in the judgment of the Board, exercises regulatory or supervisory functions with respect to any class of creditors subject to this title.

"Sec. 110. Advisory committee

The Board shall establish an advisory committee to advise and consult with it in the exercise of its functions under this title. In appointing the members of the committee, the Board shall seek to achieve a fair representation of the interests of sellers of merchandise on credit, lenders, and the public. The committee shall meet from time to time at the call of the Board, and members thereof shall be paid transportation expenses and not to exceed $100 per diem.

"Sec. 111. Effect on other laws

"(a) This title does not annul, alter, or affect, or exempt any creditor from complying with, the laws of any State relating to the disclosure of information in connection with credit transactions, except to the extent that those laws are inconsistent with the provisions of this title or regulations thereunder, and then only to the extent of the inconsistency.

"(b) This title does not otherwise annul, alter or affect in any manner the meaning, scope or applicability of the laws of any State, including, but not limited to, laws relating to the types, amounts or rates of charges, or any element or elements of charges, permissible under such laws in connection with the extension or use of credit, nor does this title extend the applicability of those laws to any class of persons or transactions to which they would not otherwise apply.

"(c) In any action or proceeding in any court involving a consumer credit sale, the disclosure of the annual percentage rate as required under this title in connection with that sale may not be received as evidence that the sale was a loan or any type of transaction other than a credit sale.

"(d) Except as specified in sections 125 and 130, this title and the regulations issued thereunder do not affect the validity or enforceability of any contract or obligation under State or Federal law.

"Sec. 112. Criminal liability for willful and knowing violation

Whoever willfully and knowingly

"(1) gives false or inaccurate information or fails to provide information which he is required to disclose under the provisions of this title or any regulation issued thereunder,

"(2) uses any chart or table authorized by the Board under section 107 in such a manner as to consistently understate the annual percentage rate determined under section 107 (a) (1) (A), or

"(3) otherwise fails to comply with any requirement imposed under this title, shall be fined not more than $5,000 or imprisoned not more than one year, or both.

"Sec. 113. Penalties inapplicable to governmental agencies

No civil or criminal penalty provided under this title for any violation thereof may be imposed upon the United States or any agency thereof, or upon any State or political subdivision thereof, or any agency of any State or political subdivision.

"Sec. 114. Reports by Board and Attorney General

Not later than January 3 of each year after 1969, the Board and the Attorney General shall, respectively, make reports to the Congress concerning the administration of their functions under this title, including such recommendations as the Board and the Attorney General, respectively, deem necessary or appropriate. In addition, each report of the Board shall include its assessment of the extent to which compliance with the requirements imposed under this title is being achieved.

Chapter 2—Credit Transactions

"Sec. 121. General requirement of disclosure

"(a) Each creditor shall disclose clearly and conspicuously, in accordance with the regulations of the Board, to each person to whom consumer credit is extended and upon whom a finance charge is or may be imposed, the information required under this chapter.

"(b) If there is more than one obligor, a creditor need not furnish a statement of information required under this chapter to more than one of them.

"Sec. 122. Form of disclosure; additional information

"(a) Regulations of the Board need not require that disclosures pursuant to this chapter be made in the order set forth in this chapter, and may permit the use of terminology different from that employed in this chapter if it conveys substantially the same meaning.

"(b) Any creditor may supply additional information or explanations with any disclosures required under this chapter.

"Sec. 123. Exemption for State-regulated transactions

The Board shall by regulation exempt from the requirements of this chapter any class of credit transactions within any State if it determines that under the law of that State that class of transactions is subject to requirements substantially similar to those imposed under this chapter, and that there is adequate provision for enforcement.

"Sec. 124. Effect of subsequent occurrence

If information disclosed in accordance with this chapter is subsequently rendered inaccurate as the result of any act, occurrence, or agreement subsequent to the delivery of the required disclosures, the inaccuracy resulting therefrom does not constitute a violation of this chapter.

"Sec. 125. Right of rescission as to certain transactions

"(a) Except as otherwise provided in this section, in the case of any consumer credit transaction in which a security interest is retained or acquired in any real property which is used or is expected to be used as the residence of the person to whom credit is extended, the obligor shall have the right to rescind the transaction until midnight of the third business day following the consummation of the transaction or the delivery of the disclosures required under this section and all other material disclosures required under this chapter, whichever is later, by notifying the creditor, in accordance with regulations of the Board, of his intention to do so. The creditor shall clearly and conspicuously disclose, in accordance with regulations of the Board, to any obligor in a transaction subject to this section the rights of the obligor under this section. The creditor shall also provide, in accordance with regulations of the Board, an adequate opportunity to the obligor to exercise his right to rescind any transaction subject to this section.

"(b) When an obligor exercises his right to rescind under subsection (a), he is not liable for any finance or other charge, and any security interest given by the obligor becomes void upon such a rescission. Within ten days after receipt of a notice of rescission, the creditor shall return to the obligor any money or property given as earnest money, downpayment, or otherwise, and shall take any action necessary or appropriate to reflect the termination of any security interest created under the transaction. If the creditor has delivered any property to the obligor, the obligor may retain possession of it. Upon the performance of the creditor's obligations under this section, the obligor shall tender the property to the creditor, except that if return of the property in kind would be impracticable or inequitable, the obligor shall tender its reasonable value. Tender shall be made at the location of the property or at the residence of the obligor, at the option of the obligor. If the creditor does not take possession of the property within ten days after tender by the obligor, ownership of the property vests in the obligor without obligation on his part to pay for it.

"(c) Notwithstanding any rule of evidence, written acknowledgment of receipt of any disclosures required under this title by a person to whom a statement is required to be given pursuant to this section does no more than create a rebuttable presumption of delivery thereof.

"(d) The Board may, if it finds that such action is necessary in order to permit homeowners to meet bona fide personal financial emergencies, prescribe regulations authorizing the modificantion or waiver of any rights created under this section to the extent and under the circumstances set forth in those regulations.

"(e) This section does not apply to the creation or retention of a first lien against a dwelling to finance the acquisition of that dwelling.

"Sec. 126. Content of periodic statements

If a creditor transmits periodic statements in connection with any extension of consumer credit other than under an open end consumer credit plan, then each of those statements shall set forth each of the following items:

"(1) The annual percentage rate of the total finance charge.

"(2) The date by which, or the period (if any) within which, payment must be made in order to avoid additional finance charges or other charges.

"(3) Such of the items set forth in section 127 (b) as the Board may be regulation require as appropriate to the terms and conditions under which the extension of credit in question is made.

"Sec. 127. Open end consumer credit plans

"(a) Before opening any account under an open end consumer credit plan, the creditor shall disclose to the person to whom credit is to be extended each of the following items, to the extent applicable:

"(1) The conditions under which a finance charge may be imposed, including the time period, if any, within which any credit extended may be repaid without incurring a finance charge.

"(2) The method of determining the balance upon which a finance charge will be imposed.

"(3) The method of determining the amount of the finance charge, including any minimum or fixed amount imposed as a finance charge.

"(4) Where one or more periodic rates may be used to compute the finance charge, each such rate, the range of balances to which it is applicable, and the corresponding nominal annual percentage rate determined by multiplying the periodic rate by the number of periods in a year.

"(5) If the creditor so elects,

"(A) the average effective annual percentage rate of return received from accounts under the plan for a representative period of time; or

"(B) whenever circumstances are such that the computation of a rate under subparagraph (A) would not be feasible or practical, or would be misleading or meaningless, a projected rate of return to be received from accounts under the plan.

The Board shall prescribe regulations, consistent with commonly accepted standards for accounting or statistical procedures, to carry out the purposes of this paragraph.

"(6) The conditions under which any other charges may be imposed, and the method by which they will be determined.

"(7) The conditions under which the creditor may retain or acquire any security interest in any property to secure the payment of any credit extended under the plan, and a description of the interest or interest which may be so retained or acquired.

"(b) The creditor of any account under an open end consumer credit plan shall transmit to the obligor, for each billing cycle at the end of which there is an outstanding balance in that account or with respect to which a finance charge is imposed, a statement setting forth each of the following items to the extent applicable:

"(1) The outstanding balance in the account at the beginning of the statement period.

"(2) The amount and date of each extension of credit during the period, and, if a purchase was involved, a brief identification (unless previously furnished) of the goods or services purchased.

"(3) The total amount credited to the account during the period.

"(4) The amount of any finance charge added to the account during the period, itemized to show the amounts, if any, due to the application of percentage rates and the amount, if any, imposed as a minimum or fixed charge.

"(5) Where one or more periodic rates may be used to compute the finance charge, each such rate, the range of balances to which it is applicable, and, unless the annual percentage rate (determined under section 107 (a) (2)) is required to be disclosed pursuant to paragraph (6), the corresponding nominal annual percentage rate determined by multiplying the periodic rate by the number of periods in a year.

"(6) Where the total finance charge exceeds 50 cents for a monthly or longer billing cycle, or the pro rata part of 50 cents for a billing cycle shorter than monthly, the total finance charge expressed as an annual percentage rate (determined under section 107 (a) (2)), except that if the finance charge is the sum of two or more products of a rate times a portion of the balance, the creditor may, in lieu of disclosing a single rate for the total charge, disclose each such rate expressed as an annual percentage rate, and the part of the balance to which it is applicable.

"(7) At the election of the creditor, the average effective annual percentage rate of return (or the projected rate) under the plan as prescribed in subsection (a) (5).

"(8) The balance on which the finance charge was computed and a statement of how the balance was determined. If the balance is determined without first deducting all credits during the period, that fact and the amount of such payments shall also be disclosed.

"(9) The outstanding balance in the account at the end of the period.

"(10) The date by which, or the period (if any) within which, payment must be made to avoid additional finance charges.

"(c) In the case of any open end consumer credit plan in existence on the effective date of this subsection, the items described in subsection (a), to the extent applicable, shall be disclosed in a notice mailed or delivered to the obligor not later than thirty days after that date.

"Sec. 128. Sales not under open end credit plans

"(a) In connection with each consumer credit sale not under an open end credit plan, the creditor shall disclose each of the following items which is applicable:

"(1) The cash price of the property or service purchased.

"(2) The sum of any amounts credited as downpayment (including any trade-in).

"(3) The difference between the amount referred to in paragraph (1) and the amount referred to in paragraph (2).

"(4) All other charges, individually itemized, which are included in the amount of the credit extended but which are not part of the finance charge.

"(5) The total amount to be financed (the sum of the amount

described in paragraph (3) plus the amount described in paragraph (4)).

"(6) Except in the case of a sale of a dwelling, the amount of the finance charge, which may in whole or in part be designated as a time-price differential or any similar term to the extent applicable.

"(7) The finance charge expressed as an annual percentage rate except in the case of a finance charge.

"(A) which does not exceed $5 and is applicable to an amount financed not exceeding $75, or

"(B) which does not exceed $7.50 and is applicable to an amount financed exceeding $75.

A creditor may not divide a consumer credit sale into two or more sales to avoid the disclosure of an annual percentage rate pursuant to this paragraph.

"(8) The number, amount, and due dates or periods of payments scheduled to repay the indebtedness.

"(9) The default, delinquency, or similar charges payable in the event of late payments.

"(10) A description of any security interest held or to be retained or identification of the property to which the security interest relates.

"(b) Except as otherwise provided in this chapter, the disclosures required under subsection (a) shall be made before the credit is extended, and may be made by disclosing the information in the contract or other evidence of indebtedness to be signed by the purchaser.

"(c) If a creditor receives a purchase order by mail or telephone without personal solicitation, and the cash price and the deferred payment price and the terms of financing, including the annual percentage rate, are set forth in the creditor's catalog or other printed material distributed to the public, then the disclosures required under subsection (a) may be made at any time not later than the date the first payment is due.

"(d) If a consumer credit sale is one of a series of consumer credit sales transactions made pursuant to an agreement providing for the addition of the deferred payment price of that sale to an existing outstanding balance, and the person to whom the credit is extended has approved in writing both the annual percentage rate or rates and the method of computing the finance charge or charges, and the creditor retains no security interest in any property as to which he has received payments aggregating the amount of the sales price including any finance charges attributable thereto, then the disclosure required under subsection (a) for the particular sale may be made at any time not later than the date the first payment for that sale is due. For the purposes of this subsection, in the case of items purchased on different dates, the first purchased shall be deemed first paid for, and in the case of items purchased on the same date, the lowest priced shall be deemed first paid for.

"Sec. 129. Consumer loans not under open end credit plans

"(a) Any creditor making a consumer loan or otherwise extending consumer credit in a transaction which is neither a consumer credit sale nor under an open end consumer credit plan shall disclose each of the following items, to the extent applicable:

"(1) The amount of credit of which the obligor will have the actual use, or which is or will be paid to him or for his account or to another person on his behalf.

"(2) All charges, individually itemized, which are included in the amount of credit extended but which are not part of the finance charge.

"(3) The total amount to be financed (the sum of the amounts referred to in paragraph (1) plus the amounts referred to in paragraph (2)).

"(4) Except in the case of a loan secured by a first lien on a dwelling and made to finance the purchase of that dwelling, the amount of the finance charge.

"(5) The finance charge expressed as an annual percentage rate except in the case of a finance charge.

"(A) which does not exceed $5 and is applicable to an extension of consumer credit not exceeding $75, or

"(B) which does not exceed $7.50 and is applicable to an extension of consumer credit exceeding $75.

A creditor may not divide an extension of credit into two or more transactions to avoid the disclosure of an annual percentage rate pursuant to this paragraph.

"(6) The number, amount, and the due dates or periods of payments scheduled to repay the indebtedness.

"(7) The default, delinquency, or similar charges payable in the event of late payments.

"(8) A description of any security interest held or to be retained or acquired by the creditor in connection with the extension of credit, and a clear identification of the property to which the security interest relates.

"(b) Except as otherwise provided in this chapter, the disclosures required by subsection (a) shall be made before the credit is extended, and may be made by disclosing the information in the note or other evidence of indebtedness to be signed by the obligor.

"(c) If a creditor receives a request for an extension of credit by mail or telephone without personal solicitation and the terms of financing, including the annual percentage rate for representative amounts of credit, are set forth in the creditor's printed material distributed to the public, or in the contract of loan or other printed material delivered to the obligor, then the disclosures required under subsection (a) may be made at any time not later than the date the first payment is due.

"Sec. 130. Civil liability

"(a) Except as otherwise provided in this section, any creditor who fails in connection with any consumer credit transaction to disclose to any person any information required under this chapter to be disclosed to that person is liable to that person in an amount equal to the sum of

"(1) twice the amount of the finance charge in connection with the transaction, except that the liability under this paragraph shall not be less than $100 nor greater than $1,000; and

"(2) in the case of any successful action to enforce the foregoing liability, the costs of the action together with a reasonable attorney's fee as determined by the court.

"(b) A creditor has no liability under this section if within fifteen days after discovering an error, and prior to the institution of an action under this section or the receipt of written notice of the error, the creditor notifies the person concerned of the error and makes whatever adjustments in the appropriate account are necessary to insure that the person will not be required to pay a finance charge in excess of the amount or percentage rate actually disclosed.

"(c) A creditor may not be held liable in any action brought under this section for a violation of this chapter if the creditor shows by a preponderance of evidence that the violation was not intentional and resulted from a bona fide error notwithstanding the maintenance of procedures reasonably adapted to avoid any such error.

"(d) Any action which may be brought under this section against the original creditor in any credit transaction involving a security interest in real property may be maintained against any subsequent assignee of the original creditor where the assignee, its subsidiaries, or affiliates were in a continuing business relationship with the original creditor either at the time the credit was extended or at the time of the assignment, unless the assignment was involuntary, or the assignee shows by a preponderance of evidence that it did not have reasonable grounds to believe that the original creditor was engaged in violations of this chapter, and that it maintained procedures reasonably adapted to apprise it of the existence of any such violations.

"(e) Any action under this section may be brought in any United States district court, or in any other court of competent jurisdiction, within one year from the date of the occurrence of the violation.

"Sec. 131. Written acknowledgment as proof of receipt

Except as provided in section 125 (c) and except in the case of actions brought under section 130 (d), in any action or proceeding by or against any subsequent assignee of the original creditor without knowledge to the contrary by the assignee when he acquires the obligation, written acknowledgment of receipt by a person to whom a statement is required to be given pursuant to this title shall be conclusive proof of the delivery thereof and, unless the violation is apparent on the face of the delivery thereof and, unless the violation is apparent on the face of the statement, of compliance with this chapter. This section does not affect the rights of the obligor in any action against the original creditor.

Chapter 3—Credit Advertising

"Sec. 141. Catalogs and multiple-page advertisements

For the purposes of this chapter, a catalog or other multiple-page advertisement shall be considered a single advertisement if it clearly and conspicuously displays a credit terms table on which the information required to be stated under this chapter is clearly set forth.

"Sec. 142. Advertising of downpayments and installments

No advertisement to aid, promote, or assist directly or indirectly any extension of consumer credit may state

"(1) that a specific periodic consumer credit amount or installment amount can be arranged, unless the creditor usually and customarily arranges credit payments or installments for that period and in that amount.

"(2) that a specified downpayment is required in connection with any extension of consumer credit, unless the creditor usually and customarily arranges downpayments in that amount.

"Sec. 143. Advertising of open end credit plans

No advertisement to aid, promote, or assist directly or indirectly the extension of consumer credit under an open end credit plan may set forth any of the specific terms of that plan or the appropriate rate determined under section 127 (a) (5) unless it also clearly and conspicuously sets forth all of the following items:

"(1) The time period, if any, within which any credit extended may be repaid without incurring a finance charge.

"(2) The method of determining the balance upon which a finance charge will be imposed.

"(3) The method of determining the amount of the finance

charge, including any minimum or fixed amount imposed as a finance charge.

"(4) Where periodic rates may be used to compute the finance charge, the periodic rates expressed as annual percentage rates.

"(5) Such other or additional information for the advertising of open end credit plans as the Board may by regulation require to provide for adequate comparison of credit costs as between different types of open end credit plans.

"Sec. 144. Advertising of credit other than open end plans

"(a) Except as provided in subsection (b), this section applies to any advertisement to aid, promote, or assist directly or indirectly any consumer credit sale, loan, or other extension of credit subject to the provisoes of this title, other than open end credit plan.

"(b) The provisions of this section do not apply to advertisements of residential real estate except to the extent that the Board may be regulation require.

"(c) If any advertisement to which this section applies states the rate of a finance charge, the advertisement shall state the rate of that charge expressed as an annual percentage rate.

"(d) If any advertisement to which this section applies states the amount of the downpayment, if any, the amount of any installment payment, the dollar amount of any finance charge, or the number of installments or the period of repayment, then the advertisement shall state all of the following items:

"(1) The cash price or the amount of the loan as applicable.

"(2) The downpayment, if any.

"(3) The number, amount, and due dates or period of payments scheduled to repay the indebtedness if the credit is extended.

"(4) The rate of the finance charge expressed as an annual percentage rate.

"Sec. 145. Nonliability of media

There is no liability under this chapter on the part of any owner or personnel, as such, of any medium in which an advertisement appears or through which it is disseminated.

Appendix VII

USING A LAWYER

When creditor negotiations are going nowhere, a lawyer can often get you the settlement you need. Once an attorney is involved, the creditor usually begins to worry about limiting liability. Most creditors are in business to make money, not to fight for the right to report derogatory credit.

Don't find your lawyer in the yellow pages. Call your Bar Association for a referral. Lawyers can be very expensive, so define the scope of your action and the pricing before working together. The consultation should be free.

A lawyer can:

• define your strongest position in a dispute;
• demand that the creditor prove it has met all its responsibilities (i.e., proper billing, notifications, and disclosures);
• make affirmative arguments under, among other laws, the Fair Credit Reporting Act, Fair Credit Billing Act, and Truth in Lending Act; as well as review the credit agreement and pursue lawsuits. These tactics put the creditor on the defensive;
• negotiate an enforceable agreement that clears your credit in exchange for ending the dispute.